America has been trying to rectify its misdeeds against certain groups within its culture: women, minorities, homosexuals and the different classes. There have been two ways to further proceed–accept it and move on or cry out victimhood and demand reparations. The former option was never even considered–so now let the trial of America begin.

VICTIMS OF

WHITE MALE

HOW VICTIM CULTURE
VICTIMIZES SOCIETY

R.C. SEELY

INTRODUCTION

Ever since the founding of this great nation, there has been a civil war going on. The time period starting in the 1800's was simply an admittance of this fact, now the war has shifted from the battlefield into the courtroom. Lawyers and the political elite are the modern day Confederacy and Union forces.

On the one side are representatives of the constitutional principles; such as Ted Cruz and Rand Paul. Representatives who are not perfect, but at least they try. On the other side, those who think they are above the Constitution; Barack Obama, Harry Reid and John McCain, to get started. One side knows their place and listens to "We the People" the other thinks that the people are "too stupid" too understand what is best for them. In their minds they have to decide for us what is best.

What's more many think that everything about this country is wrong. That because at one time our nation openly supported slavery it must be evil, in touting this line they have forgotten the true history of slavery. They have forgotten that slavery and bigotry is not an American trait, it was at the time, a *Human* trait. Pretty much every country has practiced slavery or indentured servitude. But, while the rest of the world has moved on from their racist past, the Progressives who think that we owe those who have been wronged get their reparations for our national misdeeds. The claims of racism is the subject of this book. In it I will point out the ridiculous, the times when they are partially right and the times when they were right. America is on trial, and the prosecutors are calling for blood; the blood of the White Male to be more precise.

CHAPTER ONE
COURT'S IN SESSION

Hear ye, hear ye. Court is now in session. In defense of the United States of America is R.C. Seely, against the progressives and its allies. It's now time to hear the charges.

THE INDICTMENT

The United States is charged with hate crimes against its people. Crimes against minorities, gays, women, the poor, the ugly, the smelly, the incompetent, animals and anyone else who feels emotional scarred, for any reason, whether reasonable or not. We have Eric Holder stating that "though this nation has proudly thought of itself as a melting pot in things racial ... we are a nation of cowards... We average Americans simply do not want to talk enough with each other about race... Given all that we as a nation went through during the civil rights struggle, it is hard for me to accept that the result of those efforts was to create an America that is ... voluntarily socially segregated."

President Barack Obama had this to say on that matter of race, while visiting the Turkish parliament, "The U.S. is still working through some of our darker periods in our history. Our country still struggles with the legacies of slavery and segregation, the past treatment of Native Americans." Frederica Wilson, a Florida democrat, had this to say about race, "Mr. Speaker, I am tired of burying young black boys. I am tired of watching them suffer at the hands of those who fear them. I am tired of comforting mothers, fathers, grandparents, sisters and brothers after such unnecessary, heinous crimes of violence." Eugene Robison, a writer for the *Washington Post,* addressed the issue of Trayvon Martin, like this, "Imagine that Martin, not Zimmerman, had been carrying a legal handgun and that it was Zimmerman who ended up dead. The law should have compelled police to release, a young African American in a hoodie, without charges. Somehow I doubt that would have happened."

Feminist Coral Gilligan states in her book *In A Different Voice,* "at the core of a patriarchal, racist social order [that had] ushered in an ideology and a psychology of separation as to be read as natural, normal, necessary and inevitable. The disassociation from relationship and specifically from relationship with women and from vast reaches of the inner world hid the experiences, the thoughts and the feelings of all people who were considered to be lesser, less developed, less human, and we all know who those people are: women, people of colour, gays and lesbians, the poor and the disabled." Even supreme court judge, Ruth Bader Ginsburg, commented on the victimhood of women saying that "Sex classifications may be used to compensate women 'for particular economic disabilities [they have] suffered to promote equal employment opportunity' to advance the full talent and capacities of our Nation's people. But such classifications may not be used, as they once were, to create or perpetuate the legal, social and economic inferiority of women." When the discussion does turn to boys, it still is about victim status, with experts trying to explain the actions of boys' tendencies towards violence. Dr. William Pollock, who studies the Columbine shootings said his "findings carry massive implications for what appears to be a larger national crisis, one that we are now seeing can occasion serious violence... The time has come to change the way boys are raised in our homes, in our schools and in society." Columnist Elizabeth Gleick wrote in *Time*

Magazine that she sees "dozens of troubled teenage girls troop across the pages ... who were raped, ... have bulimia, ... have pierced bodies, ... shaved heads, ... coping with strict religious families or ... their parents bitter divorce." Clinical psychologist Mary Pipher gives a similar description in her book *Reviving Ophelia,* that "her clinic is filled with girls who have tried to kill themselves."

Paul Broca, the French professor of clinical surgery of the 19th century stated that "the relatively small size of the female brain depends in part upon her physical inferiority and in part upon her intellectual inferiority." So clearly there has been some legitimacy in the feminist claim of perceived inferiority, but is this as widespread as they would have us believe?

Indiana governor, Mike Pence received a lot of criticism for his support of the Religious Restoration act, as a bill that "will ... subsidize legally-sanctioned discrimination against gay, bisexual and transgender people," according to San Francisco mayor, Ed Lee. Apple's openly gay CEO, Tim Cook reported statement was–in part–"Around the world we strive to treat every customer the same–regardless of where they come from, how they worship or who they love." Gen Con–a Seattle-based gaming group–CEO Adrian Swartout, went on to say "The message this legislature sends to tourists, Indy local and the overall business community is one of exclusion." The group brings in an estimated $50 million into Indianapolis with its convention and Gen Con has already started looking for other locations.

Activist Cornel West, has warned of a "Planetary Selma" coming from our dependency of fossil fuels, calling the Harvard University fossil fuel divestment an "ecological catastrophe ... as evil as white supremacist catastrophe, anti-gay catastrophe, anti-Muslim catastrophe."

I admit this paints a picture of America that is less than appealing, but is it a fair characterization? All right, let's have a discussion about race, and all the other aspects of Victim Culture. This submission will be made for the court of public opinion to decide. The defense will now state his case.

OPENING REMARKS

Thank you, your honor. My case is a fairly simple one: the very charges of Hate Crimes, are themselves, not reasonable by any legal definition. They violate the very premise of freedom and liberty, starting with a complete abandonment of the first amendment, placing Political Correctness over Free Speech of every kind. They don't enhance justice, but produce instead a kind of selective victimization form of justice. A version of justice based on how a whole demographic was wronged by interpretation, not on case evidence.

Simply put, Hate Crimes divide us and place emphasis on a "victim's" superficial traits; traits of race, religion, gender, sexual preference, class status, or whatever else they claim, it places their freedom over the rights of another. Making them perpetrators of the very crimes they are accusing others of committing. By their very nature, it is clear that Hate Crimes are immoral.

Why do we put up with all this Hate Crimes legislature? How did we get here? Mostly, it came out of cowardice. Cowardice from judges that are too eager to pacify the lawyers and "victims" rather than do their job and tell them an emphatic–NO! Greed from lawyers, is another big part of the equation. Lawyers without scruples will eagerly abandon their professional ethics for the grandeur and financial windfall. Popular culture plays into this as well, convincing everyone that it's not their fault–even when it clearly is. Lastly, it is we, the American people, who don't adequately make our disgust with all this mess known.

EXHIBIT A

While there are numerous cases that the

prosecutors of the nation will submit for evidence of America's guilt of apathy towards the needy and helpless, I would like to start with this one in the defense: The invention of the baby incubator.

As with many of the stories the prosecution would submit, this is another rife with emotional reactionaryism and analytical refrain. It took place during the 1800's, when a Dr. Martin Couney—eager to introduce his version of the incubator to the world—decided to step up a display at the Coney Island in New York. During the event, activists—acting on the premature children's behalf—claimed Dr. Couney was exploiting the children. They challenged him at every step of the way, but he eventually won and it's a good thing too. If not, the many premature infants that are alive today might not have had a chance at life. Surprisingly absent were the so-called "victims" parents in the protesting crowds, maybe they didn't care about their children being "exploited" if it meant they might live.

Maybe they didn't see it as exploitation at all and that, in this case, Couney was acting *for* their children and it was the protestors who were being the bullies.

The unfortunate truth is this is not uncommon at all and the more "progressive" the less progress we get.

THE SUSPECTS

The true culprits in this are always the same, the establishment republicans and the social democrats. They create the culture that encourages the cronyism and incompetence to spread like a virus and the rest of us have to suffer the consequences of this bureaucratic plague. The cure for their incompetence–they claim–is they never have enough money, how much do they need? How many taxpayer dollars will assuage their spending addiction? When will *authentic* justice and common sense become the cause in Washington? It's looking like never. With the 70,000 pages of laws the nation already has and no end in sight to that list, there is a perverse incentive to act against the best interest of the American people.

The only way to change that is for the populace to alter their thinking: instead of demanding our politicians take charge and fix things, we reach out to the community and tell the politicians to stay out of the way. Otherwise this cycle will simply continue unabated.

REASONABLE DOUBT

There is room to doubt my finding in the following defense on America's behave but much of the condemnation will be by those thoroughly entrenched in this system, that their criticism is almost laughable. Maybe you should laugh about it, let them know how amusing their system–of which can only be described as Complex Absurdity– really is. Let them know how you feel about all these frivolous lawsuits, that stifle innovation and keep great products or improvements off the market; or declare their unconditional allegiance to lobbyists and their party of the duopoly, as part of the problem and not the solution; let them know you're mad as hell and sick and tired of helping those who refuse to help themselves who can, with expensive programs built with *your hard- earned money*; or let them know that they have given you reasonable doubt in their convictions about their cause, especially when they act in a manner that violates economic principles and even the law.

If this culture of dubious victimhood, based on "hate crimes" and identity politics is ever to be disassembled, it must be done by the honest citizens, who have no financial or political gain for it to succeed. It must be done also, to ensure that future generations can get back the American dream.

HATE CRIMES, VICTIM CULTURE AND INDENTITY POLITICS

When Martin Luther King Jr. was alive and pushing for equality, he never once talked about reparations in his speeches, he talked about being proud, proud of who you are and not let others tear you down. I have a hard time believing that he would have advocated our current legislative agenda of "hate crimes" or identity politics or the Victim Culture all together. If he did there would be far less people that would have sided with him and he wouldn't be commemorated as a civil rights icon by those on the right as well as the left. "I have a dream of black children and white children playing together" doesn't resonant the same tone of "we are due" –the mantra of the civil rights movement of the twenty-first century.

It would not be an unfair assessment to conclude that the complete and total change of direction and tone in the movement today would make King cry tears of sorrow, not joy. The social democrats took everything King did and turned it around as a means to offer the populist voters a taxpayer funded, door prize for voting democrat. The sad thing is the "party of no"–the

Republicans–hasn't been saying no much lately, but more "well, we'll see." That's quite a feat standing up without a spine!

HABEUS CORPSES

Being a constitutional libertarian, I care highly about civil rights, which is one more reason why this culture of false victimhood is not only sickening, but downright dangerous. The more dubious declarations of victimhood that come out, the more people ignore the claims of legitimate grievances. The more we talk about Trayvon, the less we care about another victim with a justified claim. The more we talk about blacks being killed by white officers, the less we care about general police misconduct. The more we talk about the gender wage gap and the "War on Women", the less we care about rape and the negative effects of abortion laws. The more we focus on a medical disorder that affects thousands of people–such as ALS– the less funds and resources go to conditions that are more prevalent, with hundreds of thousands or millions suffering. See, when we have a cultural fixation on an issue, from a single perspective, the unintended consequences and other relevant points connected to the issue get ignored.

The really horrible thing is this is hardly unintentional, and this is definitely not a single party problem–at times even being done with bipartisanship. When there are legitimate concerns on issues, the party that views it as trivial will sweep all the other viewpoints under the rug. Along with the cohorts in the media and other such interests, the politician will proceed to create a bubble of compliance around themselves that protects them from harm–in their careers and from hearing about the negative effects of their legislature. They are playing god but don't know they have made a famine. Oops! Time to spin this little error of judgment and the political machine keeps on going.

JUST THE FACTS

While many legal arguments are charged with emotion, mine are reason based because I want the reader to come to their own conclusion. I will present you with the information and you can take it or leave it. *There will be no emotional manipulation here,* if you want that, read *Salon* magazine or turn on MSNBC. If you are the type who wants to learn or have an open discussion—with both views treated with equal respect, then you might enjoy this book. If you think all other opinions have no merit and don't want to hear them, you probably won't. I don't call out people because their opinions are wrong, I call them out when they can't logically defend those opinions.

WHO FRAMED UNCLE SAM?

The duopoly are responsible for the system of corruption, but they didn't act alone. In this book, I will expose the other culprits and hopefully you will see that

America was not only framed, but there

wasn't even an actual crime committed. My objective here is to expose hate crimes, identity politics and the Victim Culture, for what they truly are–legal voodoo.

CHAPTER TWO

LIVING AMONG THE ZOMBIES

Have you ever met any zombies?

They are real you know– brain-dead, collectivists who chant "yes we can" or "forward", and say stupid things like, "if only we gave the president, temporary dictatorial powers" or think the government can make better decisions for you than you can.

As you will see, the trial of America is more than just about race, the Hate Crimes and guilt charges penetrate every aspect of society. The zombies are well aware of this, they simply don't care. They know they are right and no matter how compelling and comprehensive the evidence might be they won't change their minds. While this book is full of the zombies' of our society, the ones in this chapter, these are the most relevant ones; the zombies that got Obama elected, not once but twice and sent the country on the fast lane to socialism.

WEAPON OF JACKASS DESTRUCTION

As I've mentioned previously, one of my favorite and most poignant authors is the late George Orwell, his book was the major influence for my book '*We the Rodents*' and he (amongst other famous writers, like, Kafka and Voltaire) has had influences on both the *Americanus Libertae* blog and my book *UNConventional Wisdom*. It appears that I'm not alone in my respect and appreciation for the works of Orwell, with President Obama showing a certain amount of knowledge in his manner of legislating. The major difference is that the president seems determined to test the theories of

Orwell, where I see them as a dire warning.

His vision appears to be to bring the nightmarish world of 1984 to reality, not only with the invasions of the peoples' privacy, but implementing the principles of *Newspeak*–the active role by government to destroy the meaning of words. As one MSNBC reporter intimated on her show the alias for the president's main law "Obamacare" should be considered equal to the more common derogatory term to the president's ethnic race. Making this another example of the absurd assertion that anyone who even questions the administration's ideology must be a racist –that has become the most lazy and dishonest argument by the Obama-media.

That is old news though, there's a new and more insidious line of propaganda in favor of the Affordable Care Act (ACA), but to see it more clearly we have to go back to the beginning of the "Obama-nation." During his first presidential campaign, then candidate Barack Obama said "if you like your doctor you can keep your doctor, no one is trying to take your doctor away from you," the fine print in his 2,000 plus page signature bill that he didn't tell you, is that this is only if they stay in the field. With the problems of reimbursement and guaranteed increases in costs on their patients, many doctors have left their fields. In a few cases it's been entire hospitals, including the best in the nation such as, Cedar Sinai and Sloane Kettering refusing to accept ACA patients. He also promised that costs would go down and that you could keep your insurance, also not true, almost six million people have lost their individual insurance policies due to the regulations in the Affordable Care Act. The costs of the new replacement policies have been, in many cases substantially higher, but if you pay higher that translates to better coverage right? That's the intimation of Ezekiel Emanuel and architect of the ACA said "if you want to pay more for an insurance company that covers your doctor you can do that .... you pay more for certain–for a wider range of choices or a wider range of benefits." This is a rare moment of honesty from the administration; sadly even this isn't completely true. In some states this is the case, but in most it's not–even if you pay more you *still* will likely get shafted under the new health care law.

This is another example of an Obamaian Slip; this is the opposite of a Freudian slip, where an involuntary truth slips out, but instead an involuntary lie. More Obamaian Slips were the major selling points for signing the law: That it would help seniors, that he initiated keeping youth on their parents' plan until age 26 and that it would benefit those with prediagnosed conditions.

First off, to help seniors, the system has to have a high enrollment rate by the twenty–thirty year old demographic. So let me see if I understand this, it's considered moral for the elderly–who should have been saving throughout their lives–to have their healthcare needs subsidized by the youth, who don't even have any money yet? Morally or practically, that sounds like trying to get blood from a stone. Along with those arguments there's the biggest flaw that wasn't considered–what if the youth don't enroll? Which is what has occurred and this disenfranchisement started with the HealthCare.gov website. The site had a "disappointing" rollout that was its downfall for the tech-savvy youth, think of it like this–you voted for the most new age president, who ran the most proficient and effective social media marketing campaign in history and the webpage for his trademark legislature doesn't work... this does not compute! The speculation by its proponents is that it was intentional to avoid the backlash from new enrollees having to pay for their new policies, so to stall they built a slow and inefficient webpage–intentional or legitimate incompetence, is immaterial, either way the error has caused what could be irreparable harm on the healthcare plan. The youth, who were Obama's strongest supporters, are now his harshest critics and it will be the seniors who will be paying the price for it.

So will the president take responsibility for this, and if not who will take the heat? Since he hasn't accepted responsibility for anything else under his watch, it's doubtful he'll start here. As for the promise to keep children on their parents plan until age 26, that was not Obama's idea, there were already insurance companies that offered that benefit–stop being lazy and shop around.

For those with prediagnosed conditions– they have the real potential to suffer along with the seniors, not only because specialty physicians will be leaving en mass so the quality of care will be greatly diminished, but under socialized medicine will bring about a lack of resources. With prices of medicine devices dropped, those with the money will purchase and stockpile them, so others won't have access to them, if the long lines to see a doctor don't kill them first! In Canada, there are lotteries to see who gets to see a doctor! These problems are far from speculation and have been witnessed by pretty much every country that have adopted socialized medicine, with many doctors saying they simply can't operate if they're beholden to these restrictions.

What is the driving force for all this healthcare madness? It's another symptom of the entitlement culture–you're working in a field that is based on humanitarian intentions, so it's immoral to be paid for it. Why? Doctors have families; they have bills; they have made immense sacrifices to their trade and yet, that's still not enough. The Affordable Care Act is a bad law, that's why it barely passed into law and half the country was against it then, with its numbers growing. It hasn't even been implemented and it's already harming the economy and many individuals have lost their insurance, this doesn't even include the people who will lose their employer provided coverage, which experts predict could be as high as one hundred million people... clearly the worst, is yet to come! That's why when the celebrities push for you to "get covered," I say opt out and stay naked.

HYPE AND CHALLENGES

When Barack Obama ran for president the first time, he ran on the platform of changing how Washington operates and get all the Senators and Congressmen to work together around a campfire singing and holding hands. They will all get along and the government elites–of both the parties–will make sure we all get what we deserve from government. To some this sounds like a good thing–to me this sounds like hell!

Obama was right in a couple of ways: we did get what we deserve from the government, for electing a hard-core communist/socialist sympathizer. We get expansions of already bad and inefficient federal programs and even *worse* programs; ObamaCare, ObamaPhones, expansions to the Net Neutrality and other welfare state expansions. Avoiding this is simply common sense. Obama was right about the rallying of many because of him–*just not in his favor*. Even in his own party he has lost his support, during their campaigns many democrat politicians asked the president not to tour their states because of the harm he would do to their chances of election.

Obama and his cronies on both sides will say that everyone agrees with him, whether it's environmentalism, national security, race, guns, welfare or whatever else. He makes it sounds like we are all in agreement to stifle those of us in opposition to the welfare state.

GOT EBOLA

The year of 2014 was a buzz on social media sites with the fears of Ebola, but was it warranted? Not according to doctors. The chances of getting this disease–though a horrible one–is not that easy. We should be more concerned with getting influenza, a disease that kills hundreds of thousands a year. The fear mongers in this story claim that Ebola has gone air-born and thus a plague of biblical proportions. Sorry, but I deal in evidence and not conjecture and conspiracy theories.

The only thing more bizarre than all this has been the response to it– with race agitators calling the Ebola issue *racist*! Racist? Because it's an African disease it's a black disease? This just goes to show that when it comes to people like Al Sharpton there's no claim so stupid that he won't make.

HELLO RINOS

Republican columnist and notorious agitator, Ann Coulter, wrote a scathing column calling out anyone who "voted for the Libertarian candidates" over her beloved Republican contenders. She threatened that she would "hunt down and drown" libertarian voters. A little hostile, but not unexpected from a member of the dreaded duopoly. Anyone who has the audacity to question them must be excoriated for their not conforming. Putting aside this blatant pandering to the GOP collective, it becomes a question of does and will this corroboration–by libertarians–be of benefit to the goals and ideals of their philosophy of extremely limited government? Not unless the Republican Party has learned from their past failures–which is very unlikely! It all has to do with incentives, and the republicans would have to go against their best interest–or the perceived one– depending on who you ask.

In order to understand all this you have to understand the formation of the Libertarian Party. In 1971, after the abandonment of Constitutional principles by the republican base by presidents Gerald Ford and Richard Nixon, the ardent believers in limited government power and individual choice went out on their own and founded the Libertarian Party. The political party that still favored putting the power in the hands of the person rather than the collective. So the question becomes: has there been enough of a reason for the republican base to come back to its roots? Only if they ignore the lobbyists and special interest groups and listen to the American people once again, only if they have proper cause to stop their march of Republican brand progressivism–which going by the manner in which quasi-libertarian candidates, such as Rand Paul and Ted Cruz are treated by the establishment–it looks like they are still listening to the wrong people. Which–in my opinion–means that with a vote for the R or D is still a vote for the lesser of two evils, not exactly a high endorsement of Coulter's argument.

LOUIS FARRAHKAN'S DANGEROUS TOURETTES SYNDROME

I don't understand people's blind following and devotion to Nation of Islam "spiritual leader" Louis Farrakhan. He's a total freak as far as I'm concerned. Not only is he a hard-core racial instigator, but he's not a very efficient orator–in "sermons" vibrating up and down with his hate-filled lectures. He looks more like a victim of Tourette's syndrome on steroids, than a victim of racial disparity. He also has been famous for his conspiracy theories about Jews ruling everything and started his own initiative, P.O.W.E.R.–People Organizing for Economic Rebirth–with the goal of empowering blacks to distribute products made under the *Clean and Fresh* label. He also referred to Israel as the "gutter religion" and it is "structured on injustice, thievery, lying and deceit." Along with his warped views on race and anti-Semitic sermons, his also supports L. Ron Hubbard's Dianetics, despite having no connection to Scientology. He has even gone as far as encouraging his followers to be audited by the Church of Scientology–yeah, he's completely nuts!

MICHAEL BROWN IS JESUS

After the Michael Brown shooting, just

like that of Trayvon Martin, there was a litany of extremely vocal racial agitators–stating some very odd opinions. Most of them fit nicely into the mold of Jesse Jackson and Al Sharpton: Black, male, religious leaders, with extreme views on race, but not all fit this category–take, Sarah Kinney Gaventa, a minister at St. Paul's Church in Virginia. During a sermon, she declared that God had "become Michael Brown." Equating Brown with the sacrifice for our sins, this–for obvious reasons–was not well received in the religious community especially. In part of her sermon she said:

> "In our Gospel today, standing in a center of Roman power, a town named after Caesar, Jesus asks his disciples who people say he is. Peter gets the answer right–the Messiah, the Son of the Living God."

> "The God we love came to disrupt the power structures of the world that tells us what we are worth. He is a living

God, who loved us so much and was so grieved by our inability to love him and one another, that he was willing to become human.

"He became Michael Brown. He became the victim of our sin, so we wouldn't have to sacrifice each other any more. His sacrifice should have been the last. His sacrifice was enough for us."

In reply to the contentious comments, a Virginia commentator, Rob Schilling went on record at Barbwire.com. He dismissed her statements saying she was "confused … and … such false teachings of social gospel were mentioned in the Bible." He went on to say, "God did not become Michael Brown, and Michael Brown was not a sacrifice for our sin."

THE 47% WHO WOULDN'T HAVE VOTED FOR HIM ANYWAY

Then 2012 presidential candidate Mitt Romney, made a comment stating that almost half of the American populace is on some form of government assistance. This is one remark that might have had a significant effect on his election–at least that what analysts have said, but is that true? Did it *really* cost him the election?

Doubtful, the percentage of the populace who would even be *offended* be that remark would never *dream* of voting Romney anyway. They were staunch Obama voters and only abandoned him because he *didn't give them more "free stuff."* While the evidence of Romney dismantling the welfare state or even reversing it is extremely unlikely, in fact he might have expanded on it in other ways–since he's said he's not running in 2016, this will all be academic– the perception is he is adamantly opposed to welfare and let the poor die in the streets. The thing is the evidence shows the federal "good intentions" leave the poor dying the streets, with the "war on poverty" further escalating the problems in the ghettos while throwing   more   and   more money at the problem.

"REBEL" WITH A CLUE

There's a lot of reasons to include actor Johnny Depp in this book, he's always been a strong Obama fan and he has been considered a "rebel," by some. A rebel?–By what *possible* standard could he be deemed a rebel? He fits the typical Hollywood progressive stereotype–with *one* exception: he's a gun rights advocate. That's right, he's listed in the short list–which includes, Angelina Jolie and husband Brad Pitt–that understand the importance of the second amendment and the right of self-preservation.

Other celebrities to embrace the second amendment, who you might not have heard support it are Chris Pratt–famous for his role as "Star Lord" in *Guardians of the Galaxy*–who bought his wife a firearm for her protection and his peace of mind. Actor Orland Jones from the *Sleepy Hollow* series took on the "ALS Ice Bucket Challenge" with his own twist, substituting a bucket of ammunition shells for ice water. Jones is a reserve sheriff and NRA member, who performed his version of the "Ice Bucket Challenge" t open the discussion of the Michael Brown incident. Jones was also stating that there are times when his fellow officers act inappropriately and the Brown case *might* have been one of those times. The reason I mention that is because of its relevancy to not only gun rights–but this book in general.

REVIVING THE 60'S

Most people take one of two perspectives when asked about the sixties: either, it was a time of liberation from social injustices, or the downfall of everything that made this country great. To be fair there were some very serious mistakes made and the movement of the "hippies" was not the call for liberation but one of retribution against those greedy capitalists–you know, the ones who weren't afraid to risk everything and make this world better with their inventions. Those who still idolize the movement, within the social democrats, do so because they were too young to be a part of it at the time. One of those "flower-child-wanna-bes" is our own "illustrious" president Barack Obama. While Hillary Clinton had made her mark during the Age of Aquarius, young Obama had to sit and wait. This glorification of the revolutions is what spearheads this man's entire modus operandi, he was raised by revolutionary extremists and his administration is his time to shine.

FERGUSON, MISSOURI: DEMOCRATIC PARTY HEADQUARTERS

Many actually bought the line by racial instigators, that "black lives matter" and that they care about "no justice, no peace", but in Ferguson, Missouri the truth had reared its ugly head. It was nothing more than a Democratic Party enlistment drive initiative. Rather than give real aid to the family and community of Ferguson, Al Sharpton was busy pushing the cause of the "party of people" which was apparently growing its base. The party's representatives set up Democratic Party booths to educate those there that the democrats would make sure such a thing as Michael Brown's death wouldn't happen again.

One big problem: such incidents seem to have *increased* under Obama, a *Social Democrat*! Somehow with the Democrats in, we have ended up with a series of attacks on citizens by other citizens and people–these are what exactly–anomalies? What is being ignored is that the Democrats may be eager to blame the cops, but when there's a crime being committed they–just as eagerly–turn to them to resolve it and make arrests, rather than handle it themselves. With the system of legal enforcement being–get as many arrests as possible–I don't blame Democrats skepticism toward the police, but their representatives *could* reform the system and *don't*. Rather than being angry at the police, get angry at the politicians. The Democrats are nowhere near as anti-police as they try to appear and under their administrations we will have just as many–if not more–such incidents.

A NIGHT AT THE MOVIES

Is it just me or have the movies turned hard-core activist, since the Obama administration? We have remakes of *Death at a Funeral* and *Annie* both with black casts, *The Help, Selma, Black or White, The Butler, 12 years a Slave,* just to name a few. T.V. is going the same way, with shows like *Blackish.*

Even YouTube isn't immune, Issa Rae started her career with an internet series *Awkward Black Girl* in 2011 gaining over 20 million views and over 180,000 subscribers. She grew up in Potomac, Maryland, where "things…aren't considered black," and she was "berated for 'acting white.'" She was constantly having problems trying to "fit into this blackness I was supposed to be." So she has become an activist for blackness, hiring exclusively black writers, actors and other entertainment personnel. All this considered, her comments to the *Huffington Post* are confusing, "It makes sense that diversity should be represented on television. But I do get tired of being asked to constantly speak about the black experience. If I'm writting an article, it's like, 'Hey we love your writing, we just want to talk to you about being black and why you're mad about it.' And that's frustrating. I'm like, what if I'm not mad today?" If you didn't want to talk about it, why did you bring it up? I don't start talking about the failures of popular culture and then say let's change the subject. Rae is a niche performer, who made a conscious decision to join in the racial polarity debate, if she wants to stop now go ahead. There are consequences of that decision, though.

This is a reflection of reality that can be seen when you hear a celebrity speak–it's all about civil rights, the "pay gap," or some other form of "injustice" rather than a relevant speech on the events. The moral here I guess would be, being a pop culture zombie means that it's not rude to ignore decorum, facts are irrelevant, you are a rebel when you *really* attempt to protect others' civil rights and the sixties rock!

CHAPTER THREE

VICTIMS OF BLACK (AND WHITE) FEMALES

While the feminist movement **might** have done good for society and women in the past, like so many social movements they have lost their way–this has, in turn created their own irrelevance. Men might not be gentlemen but just because you're a woman, it doesn't mean you're a lady. The actions of feminists don't make exceptions for good guys or bad guys, if you're a male you're their enemy. If you are expecting mercy from them you are in for an unpleasant surprise.

HILLARY IN THE WHITE HOUSE

Is there going to be another Clinton administration? I hope not, because the next Clinton White House wouldn't be *anything* like the first, which as far as presidents go wasn't all that bad. Yes, there were ethics violations, but as for policy (with the exceptions, of tax increases and the Brady bill) by and large didn't hurt the country, especially compared to the next two administrations.

If the Hillary Clinton White House was like Bill Clinton's, I would be far less worried, but it would be closer to the Obama White House only instead of racial exceptions it would be on feminist lines. More of the War on Women hyperbole; more taxpayer funded abortions, which the ACA already increased to 115,000 annually. Under HillaryCare it will probably be *double* that. Under the Hillary version of HUD we'll probably get government housing for all and the entire United States will be one big ghetto.

SOMETHING'S MISSING

Most of us are familiar with the case of Lorena Bobbitt, the woman that in the 1990's attempted to make her husband a eunuch, but I'll bet you don't know the *full* story in this bizarre case. So first let's go with what we know of the case: This woman was reported as an abused wife, who after years of abuse snapped and dismembered him, problem is, that's not what happened.

To start off with she wasn't being abused, at least there was no evidence of abuse. Her claims of "abuse" were based on being generally dissatisfied with the couple's sex life. I'm not sure that that is a valid form of abuse. The abuse charges were statements made by the feminists to later report it. So why did she do it? If not for abuse, what *possible* excuse could she have for committing a very extreme case of assault? There was none. No, REALLY. She gave NO justification for her actions. She simply had an "irresistible impulse" and acted on it. That's disturbing, but it gets worse. Not only does she get canonized by the feminists, but she gets away with the crime. The jury acquitted her based on grounds of insanity supposedly brought on by Post Traumatic Stress Disorder from the abuse. The *un*-proven abuse. After 45 days of psychological observations, she is released.

Now, I think domestic violence on *either* side is inexcusable and just plain cowardly, but I don't see this case as being an example of this. This is a case of a possible victim getting a pass for an even more inexcusable act. Lorena *might* have been the victim of an abusive spouse–and the statements of both of the Bobbitt's and other witnesses *do* support these claims–but why does this give *her* a free pass for assault? What if it had been reversed and she was abusive and he snapped, giving Lorena a mastectomy? Would his claims be given the same consideration because he's a man, or would he be sitting in a jail cell? Anyone who thinks that he wouldn't be in chains if things were the other way around is extremely naive, but I commend you for your thinking.

If John Bobbitt really did abuse his wife then he should have been properly judged in a court of law, not by a mentally unstable spouse. The intimation here is that she was made unstable from PTSD by her abuser, so she shouldn't have to be held responsible for her actions, but what if she was already unstable? These immediate assumptions of guilt or innocence, based on certain words— rather than getting all the facts and basing their decision on the facts—is dangerous. It means all you have to do is play the system and you can get away with pretty much anything. Lorena Bobbitt should be incarcerated for what she did, she a legitimate threat to society, however, if John Bobbitt was proven to be abusive he too is a threat and should be behind bars.

John Bobbitt wound up capitalizing on his misfortune and didn't end up permanently neutered, but the same can't be said for common sense and the criminal justice system, that let at least one, if not two mentally unstable individuals off the hook.

A FREE VASCETOMY (NATIONAL CASTRATION DAY)

Our next extreme activist probably held up Lorena Bobbitt as her role model. She goes by the title "Femitheist" and this twenty-something, thinks she has all the answers (as most dumb kids do) and her radical proposal is to have the entire male species sterilized–with the exception of a few "breeders" to make sure the human race doesn't go extinct. Girls like her–and I do mean "girl" and not woman because of the prepubescent angst demonstrated here–hate all men and treat every guy like the prom date who doesn't call after the post-event nookie.

The thought process at work here is neither sophisticated or logical, but sophomoric and emotionally-charged, with sentiments so anger infused only Kathy Griffin or Lady Gaga could truly appreciate. She's a pain in the ass of our nation and bat-crap crazy, and that's being generous. Critical feminists would probably dismiss this as my simply looking out for my own "interests," but that's not all, this "activist" is looking to justify assault for being wronged–the major difference is the scale and proximity to the perpetrator. In the case of the "femitheist" the whole male race wronged her, as is the thought process of most feminists.

Dr. Christina Hoff Summers, exposes this as bogus in her book *The War Against Boys*, "the description of America's teenager girls as silenced, tortured, voiceless and otherwise personally diminished is indeed dismaying... The malaise that comes closest to matching the symptoms mentioned by the crisis writers is a mood disorder called dysthymia .... characterized by low-esteem, feelings of inadequacy, depression, difficulty ... making decisions and social withdrawal," Summers findings were contrary to the feminist mantra though. "It [dysthymia] occurs in both sexes among children, and while it is more common in adult women than men … no more than 3 or 4 percent of the population suffers from it." Does this mean anything to those afflicted with the feminist mass hysteria? That's highly unlikely that they will ever read Summers' book, which is a shame since they will spend their lives trying to discredit it.

CLEANLINESS IS CLOSER TO WHITENESS

Celebrities have a bad habit of not thinking before they speak, take what happened to Naya Rivera of the show *GLEE* on her appearance on the *View*. She was trying to impress everyone with her knowledge of the issues and was discussing what a doctor had said about how often we should shower, in the conversation she made the comment that "showering more than once a day or every other day is such a white thing." This did not go over well with the black community. One of the Tweets she received read: "Now white people gonna

think we don't shower cuz of Naya Rivera."
I wouldn't put too much energy on this and
be more concerned on what white people
will think about your atrocious Ebonics
spelling!

Rivera went on clumsily trying to explain
herself with a theory, "I am now married to
a white man [Ryan Dorsey], and he showers
a lot. Like, a lot–two, three times a day." So
she marries a germaphobe and concludes
this is a reflection of *all* white people. In an
even more clumsy effort to defend her point
she continues with "a study says ... a
dermatologist says you are only supposed to
shower once or twice every three days, so
I'm right on the mark."

The next day Rivera went back on the
show to try to correct this error claiming she
"had an opinion on it that was supposed to
be a joke. Apparently it didn't go over so
well."

SEXUAL HARASSMENT LAWS BREEDS MORE HARASSMENT

As with many of the other progressive policies, sexual harassment laws don't solve the problem they claim to and instead breed new ones. "Harassment speech" laws detach us from society because it makes us hesitate in our interactions with others. The reason behind the laws are not unreasonable, women want to feel safe to work. They don't want to be constantly hit on. But the sacrifices for this have to be considered and whether we want to go to the extremes of the legal system to accomplish this goal.

While uncivil behavior should be discouraged, that's not what the purpose of the legal system is—it's to help those who have suffered intentional and malicious harm by others, not to act as enforcers of civility. You don't have the right to civil actions by others, but you are protected in yourself and your possessions, and if it escalates to physical harm *then* you have the right to legal recourse. As unpopular as it might be to say this, any type of enforcement is an invitation for legal abuse and interference by federal and state agencies in a businessman's privacy. How someone runs their business–as long as their actions don't harm others–is *their* business alone. The best piece of advance: if someone at work is harassing you, ignore them; report them; or find another job, but don't invite the government into your business.

TOTALLY OWNED

No one has more damage to the popular culture consensus than Oprah Winfrey, first with her insipid talk show and now with her own channel OWN. She imbibes and promotes all the worst traits of black feminism. Simply look through the shows on her network, programs that reflect dependence and racial and feminist injustices. One is putting the focal point on the personal problems of celebrities who need someone else to "fix their life." Another is the hard, strong black woman who is less than a "Sweetie Pie" and her family.

Her worst tragedy to society is her enabling of Tyler Perry including his racial, feminist and class warfare soap operas "For Better or Worse", "The Haves and the Have-Nots", "The Single Moms Club", and "If Loving You is Wrong."

WISHED FOR A LITTLE GIRL

In the collective consciousness of popular culture there is an attitude that boys are rowdy, trouble makers that have an affinity for mud, cuts and bruises; and little girls are princesses, who only want to play house and Barbie. Feminist Coral Gilligan describes the different ways the sexes deal with moral dilemmas, with women applying an "ethic of care" in line with their higher emotional sensibilities; as opposed to men who employ an "ethic of justice" congruent with abstract principles. Where this came from is not entirely clear but I'll tell you it's not true, at least not the attitude that only boys fight and cause trouble. Even those little princesses can hold their own against their siblings.

While there are fundamental differences between the sexes that start from the moment that extra chromosome is introduced (or not), genetics and environment also are factors in whether the child will be aggressive or submission in their relationship with their siblings. There could be some truth with the statement that boys are more the rough-housers, because of the testosterone; but it is an exaggeration to say that girls are innocent and don't fight. It could even be dangerous for women really, because that attitude is what probably encourages violence against the so called "weaker sex." It's not that girls are weaker by any means or innocent, far from it, it's that little girls are more subtle. Daniel Goleman, author of Emotional Intelligence explains: "Because girls develop language more quickly than ... boys ... [girls are] more experienced at articulating their feelings... This leads to a more subtle aggressiveness ... girls become more adept than boys at artful aggressive tactics like ostracism, vicious gossip and indirect vendettas… Boys, by and large, simply continue being confrontational when angered, oblivious to these more avert strategies." Girls aren't innocent, they are simply craftier.

For a long time even considering there was a biological difference between the sexes was taboo. Thankfully we have broken through that hurdle, at least to a degree. Feminists still deride anyone who does research on this. Francine Prose of the *New York Times* tells us why, in an article she explains, "by concentrating on girls ... new studies avoid the muddle of gender comparisons and the issue of whether boys experience a similar 'moment of resistance' (normal adolescent questioning). Gilligan and her colleagues are simply telling us how girls sound at two proximate but radically dissimilar stages of growing up." Thankfully some researchers care more about the truth than being liked, neuroanatomist, Laura

Allen concludes that, "as I began to look at the human, I kept finding differences. Seven or eight of the ten structures ... turned out ... different between men and women." One of the major fears for feminists is male scientists will come to the same conclusion as Paul Broca, that women are "biologically inferior" some might, but many won't. Neuroscientists Bennett and Shaywitz of Yale, using an MRI studied the brains of nineteen men and nineteen women performing a simple linguist task of matching rhyming words. The frontal cortex of the left hemisphere lit up in both genders, but in majority of the women part of the right hemisphere did as well and none of the sample of men reacted this way. In doing a forbidden research we may have discovered why women hold an advantage in language, that's not a handicap at all, much to the chagrin of feminists everywhere.

NO MORE RECESS

In a further effort to "change" boys

and all mankind is the moratorium of recess, feminists are adamant in the assertion that the actions of little boys will lead to them being future rapists or abusers of women. According to Anthony Pellegrini, a professor of early-childhood development, they are completely wrong and are exacerbating the problem they wish to correct. "The rough-and-tumble play fighting … is often confused with aggression. Wrestling around and play fighting is actually critical for the socialization skills and development" and that, "children who engaged in R&T (Rough and Tumble), typically boys tended to be liked and to be good social problem solvers." Those who did not participate in R&T play, become socially isolated and aggressive–the bullies. With the elimination of recess, aggression will become an issue. Carol Kennedy, a principal in Missouri, told the *Washington Post*, "We do take away a lot of opportunity to do things boys like to do … be rowdy, run and jump and roll around. We don't allow that." Boston teacher, Barbara Wilder-Smith reports that, "mothers and female teachers … believe that the key to producing a nonviolent adult is to remove all conflicts–toy weapons, wrestling, shoving, and imaginary explosives and crashes–from a boy's life." Other schools, in Philadelphia, for example instituted "socialized recesses" with rigid structured activities. "Recess," reported the New York Times, "become so anachronistic in Atlanta that the Cleveland Avenue grammar school … was built … without a playground."

DIFFERENT DECISIONS, DIFFERENT PAY

One of the biggest feminist fixations is that of the "wage gap" for women. They assert that it's morally wrong that a woman makes 0.77 for every dollar a man makes, if you ignore the facts and rely only on this single piece of information the anger would be justified. This is not the *whole story* however. The reliability of the dollar figure discrepancy is the first issue, it hasn't been proven and all indications show it was manufactured on the fly. Let's move on to the moral question of the debate, here's a typical hiring scenario:

Two people apply for the same position, one a thirty year old male with a   wife and a couple of kids, the other a single pregnant woman without a reliable babysitter.

Who would you hire? If you were acting as an honest steward for your business, acting in the welfare of your company first– as you should–it would be the guy. This has nothing to do with gender discrimination and everything to do with practical decision making. The guy has a marital partner to share the duties with regards to the children, so there's a less of a chance of him taking a lot of time off from work. Even if he wasn't a family man with his age, he's far less likely to call out as much as an eighteen year old, of either gender. Chances are when he does decide to pursue a family it won't affect   him   as   it would a woman, if anything he would only work harder to provide for his growing family.

Now the female applicant is already providing a reason for the employer to hesitate, she's going to be absent a lot because of her condition; she's going to be absent due to doctor appointments and being sick—a possible major complication at work, especially if it's a small business. If she works for a large company, that employs many people her absence won't be felt, but a local business with only a couple dozen employees—will leave a serious void. She simply won't be worth the risk. Even if she weren't a single mother, women—in general—don't stay in the job market as long as a man. That's the real reason men get the higher salaries, they are less of a risk. A man will start a family and stay with job because of expediency, women largely will leave their job for their family.

FROM HOGWARTS TO THE U.N. WOMEN

Emma Watson has had quite a career.
Starting out as an obnoxious know-it-all in
the Harry Potter franchise and now as a real
life know-it-all for the United Nations. Her
new goal, is the same stagnant agenda of the
U.N. of getting the "wage gap" filled, and
the HeForShe campaign is how Miss
Watson is contributing to this. To do that I
checked out the HeForShe campaign that
the former prepubescent witch-let Watson is
pushing. What you should know for starters
the full title for the downloadable documents
it is the U.N. Women Solidarity Movement
for Gender Equality ACTION PAC and this
12 page document gives you the details to
set up your very own indoctrination clinics.
Don't believe me?–Then look inside.

From the ACTION PAC documents:
**Gender equality liberates not only women
but also men from prescribed social roles
and gender stereotypes.** *Prescribed social
roles, I'm a guy so I have a disease?
According to the UN that's what it sounds
like.* **It is time to capitalize on the**

recognition that women's empowerment is essential for inclusive economic growth, social cohesion and social justice, environmental balance, and for progress in all spheres of life... men and boys need to be a part of the global movement to promote women's rights both as advocates and stakeholders, who need to change to make gender equality a reality for all. *So, in other words, women don't need men, but they need men to make this change happen? That's a little confusing, or am I alone here?*

But also what if a man doesn't want to change or doesn't buy into all this–what then, will he be cast out of the human race? They don't say, so that will have to remain a mystery for now. This is not about women or men, it is about crafting a shared vision of human progress...a solidarity movement...for...gender equality. The success of the HeForShe international solidarity movement requires the full participation of the UN entities and their country offices... **The success of this international movement requires the full participation of all society in particular youth... The HeForShe campaign will support and challenge the youth to contribute to advancing gender equality as agents of change.** *Yes, I want to be an agent of change. Yes, I will do whatever Hermione Granger says.*

Our goal is to mobilize *"one billion men by July 2015"* **to help communities around the world develop sustainable and transformative programs to promote gender equality.**

Oh, you can't leave yet! You haven't donated. **EQUAL PAY #78 cents Make up the difference. I believe that we are all equal and should have equal pay for equal work. Yet my female co-workers in the US still make 78 cents for every dollar I make. Today I am making up the difference by donating 22% of my income for the day.** *What if you are the one on the lower end of the pay scale and you're a guy,* *will they stand up for you? Unlikely.*

Maybe I'm in workplaces that are the exception–but I haven't seen most of my women co-workers work as hard as the men and many leave certain tasks, because they are "men's work." When I see women change their habits as well, *then* I will support these kinds of movements. This movement has other celebrity endorsements as well, here's the one by Matt Damon, "It's an objective fact, that if you want to solve some of the huge, king of bigger problems of extreme poverty, you have to include the women. They're the ones who will get it done."

THINK IN PINK

The "pink is for girls" social association is far more recent than most of us knew, it didn't even start to take hold in the culture until the 1950's. Historian Jo Paoletti, explains that, "there was no gender-color that held true everywhere," in a *Life's Little Mysteries* interview. The infant's trade magazine *Earnshaw's Infants' Department*, reported, in their June 1918 issue:

> "There has been a great diversity of opinion on this subject, but the generally accepted rule is pink for the boy and blue for the girl. The reason is that pink, being a more decided and stronger color, is more suitable for a boy; while blue, which is more delicate and dainty is prettier for the girl."

"There was a 1927 chart in Time Magazine where department stores in various cities were contacted and asked what colors they used for boys and girls," Paoletti says. The chart showed boys in pink. The contemporary color stigma of "pink for girls" didn't start until after WWII and didn't take hold until the 1980's. How is this tied into Victim Culture? This is admittedly speculative on my part, but the timing that this reversal was advanced at the beginning of the progressive era, gives a feeling of

"Women's Empowerment." This follows the course of history, since in the lifetime of FDR it was common for boys to wear dresses so they were "gender neutral" a practice that changed after the War, as little boys wanted to dress more like their father. In come the sixties and the feminists, who wanted to go back to unisex dress with the women now wearing pants. If my speculation is the case, it's the least of the worries for the men of the human race.

WHATEVER HAPPENED TO DADDY?

The biggest problem in the most poverty stricken parts of the country isn't a lack of money thrown at it, it's the lack of parental involvement. It's far too common for fathers to abandon their children and leave the mother to fill in. This can be pointed to government programs that provide the incentive of more money if daddy leaves. The costs of this kind of program have been enormous to the black communities, having proof positive that it is connected to crime in the urban areas.

This is not the only the only concern of this sort common in the urban areas, there is also the idea of the "baby daddy." For those of you unfamiliar with this, it's an act that a woman will look for a successful man–most likely with family–and seduce him, intentionally get pregnant and try to get him to leave his family to raise their bastard child. The reason they go after a married man is mostly because he has shown to be responsible, by sticking around–ironically, turning someone who was faithful into a cheater which is what they were trying to avoid. You might be thinking that I'm letting the guy off the hook here, that's not it at all. No matter your view on premarital sex, *after* making those vows you should honor them. The man in these cases should be held responsible–accepting all ramifications from these, including legal ones–but, so should the woman who encouraged his infidelity. This is not a casual thing but a cold, calculated plan that breaks up families and has caused detrimental harm to society. As sociologist David Blanken wrote in his book *Fatherless America*, "the wealth of evidence increasingly supports the conclusion the fatherlessness is a primary generator of violence among young men." He adds. "There are exceptions, of course. But here is the rule. Boys raised by traditionally masculine fathers generally do not commit crimes. Fatherless boys commit crimes." Similar sentiments were echoed by then Senator Daniel Patrick Moynihan in, 1965, "A community that allows a large number of young men to grow up in broken families, dominated by women, never acquiring any stable relationship to male authority, never acquiring any rational expectations about the future–that community asks for and gets chaos."

The last point for consideration when it comes to the "absentee father" has to do with the unscrupulous actions of adoption agencies, when a lovechild is born. In some states, after the mother gives birth and daddy's not around, they encourage the mother to put up the child for adoption without notifying the father of the child to begin with. If the father is willing and able to provide for the child, *he should be given the opportunity.* If this had anything to do with protecting the mother or was in the best interest of the child, than the chance to go to court to prove how unfit a father he would be should be welcomed. This is simply a bad law that doesn't stop a father from being derelict, but makes him one.

CHAPTER FOUR

BULLYING THE BULLIES

When you take on the bully it's **difficult to** not become one yourself. The following are men and women who had the best of intentions, but the worse actions. They forgot that the best way to solve these problems is with community diligence not federal overreach.

BILL O'REILLY IS LOOKING OUT FOR YOU UNLESS YOU DISAGREE WITH HIM

On the flipside of the victim culture is the moralist, the people of some higher intellect who are "looking out for you," by inhibiting you because your exercise of freewill violates their personal virtues and sensibilities. Bill O'Reilly is one of the most vocal–and at times most dangerous–of these individuals. One of the traits that make them so dangerous is a fundamental lack of humility and curiosity. They don't ask open questions, but ones that fit their perspective. They don't even consider they might be wrong or even acknowledge the microscopic possibility they are wrong.

How is that any different than what you do?–My critics might ask. Well for starters, I've never said I'm absolutely right. I say *all the time*, I might be wrong, I try to limit that by reading up on the topic covered as much as possible. A moralist like O'Reilly might sift through the data only not to get a "fair and balanced" argument, but the argument that strictly conforms his point of view. If you think this is an unfair analysis of the pundit look at how he treats his guests, sometimes they have it coming, when he's trying to get an answer to the question asked and the guest is determined to divert the conversation to the tangent they want. That is ethically appropriate behavior, it is finding the truth in the lie, but at times O'Reilly gets this wrong and is simply trying to deny opposing opinion.

When he does this he goes from steward for the people to a pompous blowhard bullying someone who came on the show on good faith expecting their opinions being heard and respected. You can respect their right to a contrary opinion and show your disapproval of it. O'Reilly doesn't call his guests out on simply being factually wrong–or dishonest–but because they dare to disagree with him! He doesn't want to have a debate, he wants them to submit. This is made evident by his general attitudes on issues which collectively have called for an attitude of paradoxical philosophy of apathy and legislative aggressive vigilance in tandem. He doesn't care if consenting adults smoke marijuana but there needs to be a law prohibiting it. He doesn't have a problem with first amendment rights being violated as long as the children are sheltered, isn't that the *parents'* responsibility? Besides, isn't part of protecting the children making sure the right of free speech itself is protected?

SENIORS AND SMART PHONES

There's been a stereotypical view of seniors who are just cranky old men and women, out of touch with the world and railing against the changing times. For some this is true, but others are just as engaged and tech-savvy as the millennials. How many times have you encountered a senior relative on Facebook? There's actually quite a few. Just like there are a few of the youth that want to avoid technological changes. It appears that this has more to do with individuals than failed demographics. These stereotypes hold an amount of harm for seniors though, as they are seen as easy marks. In an investigation by the Las Vegas local news, *8 On Your Side* team there was a scammer who admitted as much. In commercials by insurance company Esurance, the company further spread this myth by showing seniors trying to understand such social media as Facebook and Twitter, as well as the online game of Candy Crush–all failing to grasp the nuances of it.

The odd thing, to me in all of this is the way that seniors tend to talk about social media. They hate it! They think it's just horrible that the kids are stuck to the cell phones, tablets and computers–all the while not seeing the hypocrisy they exhibit. How many hours do *they* spend on social media?– showing pictures of their children and grandchildren. Talking about who has died. Griping about how bad things are while romanticizing the "good old days." What is the message here? It's only a waste of time if it doesn't fit *their* definition of importance? There is a lot of stupid and trivial things on the net, but that's what popular culture is in many cases. Yes, there's a lot of porn and other dirty material, but no one is *forcing* you to engage in it and search engines and your devices have settings on them to monitor what comes on your computer. Point is that between the culture perceptions of the elderly and their blasting of modern technology–while using said technology, no less–has created a vacuum for social predators. On the internet, the laws of nature are in play, target the really young and the really old, they will put up the least resistance. Those same forms of technology have made life easier for us all, including the "grumpy old men."

HASHTAG YOU!

I always have found it a bit perplexing how some people come to the conclusions about technology. Bill O'Reilly and Stephen King, are two of the people that come to mind first. Both have made drastically absurd comments condemning our greatest accomplishments with their moral vagueness.

O'Reilly, with his reckless eagerness to

abandon civil rights because the existence of freedom of speech offends his sensibilities. His war on rap music and violent media is far more dangerous than the social consequences of either media, because he would violate others' free expression, in the name of "protecting the children" no less. Many have called for restrictions of free speech for this reason and the evidence to support such actions are dubious at best. Most studies that O'Reilly has stated are loaded with virtuous biases and fall far from proving much of anything with real certainty.

Author Stephen King's objection to technology is also extremely cliché but his does have more *facts* to support it. He believes that technology will eventually lead to the extinction of all mankind. He doesn't mean like the atomic bomb or anything like that, but more along the lines of the premise of the *Terminator* or the *Matrix*, with the machines turning us into our slaves.

Many technology analysts do agree with

King on this, that with the advancement of Artificial Intelligence and robotics, this is considered a possibility. But King takes the discussion even further, condemning *all* technology as evil. He hates cell phones and common appliances, rather odd stance for two people who rely on it so fully. I'm sure both authors only use legal pads and typewriters for writing and have someone else type it and O'Reilly never uses spellcheck. Yeah, right.

These are just two of the more public figures who have contempt for technology, but to be fair most other critics have issues with specific pieces of advancement and not technology as a whole. Many have been critical of the internet and activism on it.

When Michelle Obama went onto twitter with a cardboard sign to "Save our Girls", she incurred the wrath of many other people coining the term "Armchair Activism." To be fair, for the first lady–or any other political leader for that matter–to act in this manner is, in one word, cowardly. For the common man this is a very efficient way of getting your viewpoint known and to discourage them from such actions is irresponsible.

Another criticism of internet activism is the anonymity, it bothers many people how others conduct themselves with a lack of decorum due to the encouragement of no punishment from their actions. REALLY!! Read your history; our founders put aside their gentlemanly manners and employed downright brutal tactics, at times, to get their point across. They tarred and feathered English guards and Tories. They attacked the ships coming into port. While I agree that activists do get carried away with their actions at times–so performing dramatic, for lack of a better word "theatrical plays" rather than trying to engage in a meaningful dialogue–the only thing that would be worse still, would be to try to restrict their activism. Their anonymity is a very powerful weapon, which should *not* be curtailed simply because it may be offensive to someone's sensibilities. If O'Reilly really wants to do something to help protect the children, he should be defending their rights to free expression, not encouraging more laws to violate it.

RAP IT UP

One of the biggest contemporary trends is the push into music, not simply producing recordings of spiritual hymns and similar concerts, but also infusing their values into more mainstream genres–and some of the rock bands, such as Creed and Fly Leaf are pretty good! Some are just mediocre or preachy, but at least one of these bands is just plain dangerous. They are a Christian rap group, yes you read that right–a *Christian RAP* group! The same music that is famous for its racist overtones, misogynist lexicon, vulgarity and class warfare–in a band of piety.

While there probably are true Christian rappers who really do espouse these views of virtues, the group I'm referring to most certainly *does not*. In at least one of their songs they abdicate physical violence and assault– because of a hug, it's referred to as a "Full Frontal" hug to be exact. Basically, the claim is that a hug between two people– of the gender you're attracted to–is morally wrong because it could cause arousal. In their minds this abdicates physical violence, let me rephrase this for full impact –"I'll crack your head in, in *His* name all because of a hug!" Imagine getting your ass kicked– for *hug*! Who agrees that this is more than a little imbalanced? Or maybe it's just *they* who are out of balance! Here's the thing, the theory this is based on is seriously flawed. It ignores physical attraction and alienates us because of possible physical arousal. Physical contact is important for humans and continual recitation of such an extreme overreaction has already caused social harm–as these musicians and their listeners have shown.

When I hear of people using the excuse that media caused them to act a certain way–in a manner contraindicated to civil society–normally I just laugh it off, but due to the passions that are inflamed by religion or politics   in this case keeping an eye on these guys is appropriate.

BAN "BAN BOSSY"

I hate the "ban bossy" campaign all it ever was, was a bipartisan part of the 'War on Women" movement. The only agenda of it was to circumvent the first amendment, or should I say *another* attempt to circumvent the first amendment. The sad thing is, although most of the War on Women failed, this did get a little bit of traction, with support from both republicans and democrats, including Condoleezza Rice. But it needs to be reminded that simply because someone says something that hurts your feelings doesn't mean you have the right to censor them and maybe if others called you "bossy" the fault was on you, not them. Ever consider that before calling yourself a victim? If being called Bossy is such a bad thing, take a look at where those who were called that are now and maybe you'll see it was not only not a bad thing but a type of motivation.

CRYBABIES OFF THE FIELD

One of the stupidest things I ever heard in the news was the on-going tirade of "mean" twitter posts between football players and how they are being "harassed" by their fellow teammates. Seriously... has this country *really* gotten that pathetic in the realm of Victim Culture? The very notion that the most raw symbol of masculinity, has fallen into the trap of the "society's victim" tautology is most definitely a sign of concern. Hearing on the news, grown men spouting off that they feel like high school girls in the locker room. Essentially they've turned into *Carrie– they're all gonna laugh at you!* Maybe they should laugh at these whiners too–make an example, of how incredibly *stupid* this "I'm a victim" mantra has become.

For the record, I hate bullies, the bigger child taking others school lunch money. The girls' catty behavior, talking bad about one of their "friends" behind her back–which is a behavior far *too* many women never out-grow. In the larger scale, the actions of people like, Mao, Stalin or Hitler. But a group of professional athletes, who have to endure constant ridicule by their coach and his staff; vicious emails by zealous fans of rival teams; sports reporters openly mocking them: a few critical comments from the other players sounds like par for the course. So, man up and stop your whining like a little girl!

HEY FATTY

While celebrities can be a bit "touchy" about certain subjects and react badly because of their elevated social strata, one issue I do have to agree with them on is they do tend to get mistreated by the press. Because "the world has to know" celebrities in our culture basically forfeit their rights of privacy for their stature, hounded by the paparazzi, these leaches of the media look for the worst photos of them to display for all the world.

Many times this includes unfair scathing treatment that actors and musicians, unlike athletes, are unaccustomed. The comments about women such as Kate Upton, Jennifer Love Hewitt and Jennifer Lawrence, in reference to their weight and figures in general. Most people would agree that from a purely physical standard, these three would be among the top on feminine beauty, but listening to the way some of the social piranhas from the fashion industry regard them–it's no wonder why women and girls could feel down on themselves from magazines. If they are called "fat" by these people what chance does the average woman or girl have? Well, a little insight into this brand of writer is in order. They're not normal. First, they probably have serious esteem issues and can now address that by calling Kate Upton the colloquial term "full figured" –translation: she's fat. Most of these comments comes from an anorexia advocacy group, so too much stock shouldn't be given to their opinions anyways.

In this issue Jennifer Lawrence wasn't going to back down, good for her. She has been very vocal about it says it should stop, even if that means making a law against it. Yeah, not so good. I agree with her that they were in the wrong, but so is what *she* is suggesting. Besides if she and Upton are considered so fat why were so many eager to see their leaked nude photos? Both invasions of privacy were wrong but that doesn't mean making *another* law will make things right.

NOT ALL MUSLIMS ARE MURDERERS OR CHRISTIANS SAINTS

Not all Muslims endorse the insanity of the "mainstream" Muslim activists in America, that Muslims are in fact advocates of peace. That's what I hear from the believers of the faith and their supporters.

They might be right, I don't know for certain since I haven't read the Koran. Another common defense is that while they are militant in nature, so too is Christianity at times, so believers in that faith have no room for judgment. That's true, the early days of Christianity–here in America and abroad–is full of their zealous improprieties; racial genocides, against the Indians and Pagan religions; lootings of treasures of the tribes of the areas; lynching of former slaves; the Salem Witch trials, and European witch hunts; and murders of other Christians by *another* variant of Christianity, all were done for their faith. There is one major difference, however, Christianity has settled down, follows of Muhammad have *not*.

The rampant deaths from the Ku Klux Klan and the American Nazis are no more, now it's "honor killings" and sharia law. Now it's a man beheading his coworkers because they wouldn't convert to Islam. Now it's killing women for reporting their rape or not being fully covered. Now it's death for being gay. Now it's death for those who *don't believe* as they do, instead of because they don't look like you. Neither is right in any stretch of the imagination and violates any reasonable interpretation of theological doctrine. What's more weird is that the party of tolerance so eagerly embraces such intolerance. As bad as it may be for the democrats to support the removal of a religious statue, this is far worse than that– literally, life and death–more serious! It's puzzling that they would be so worked up at *republicans* for violating the rights of women, homosexuals and minorities, but if it's in the name of Islam that's okay.

BULLIES AREN'T SO BAD

Bullies get a bad rap, but that's because we have such a skewed interpretation of what a bully is, those who ask others for help to solve their problems and turn to the community instead of the government, not a bully; those who ask pertinent questions about how their tax dollars are being spent, not bullies; those who ask that when a white man is hurt by a minority be treated the same, not a bully; and those who have serious reservations about people who claim they kill in the name of their God, are not bullies either. Do you see the pattern? You ask a question you get called a bully, or racist, sexist, homophobe, Islamophobic, or some other type of phobe that hasn't been created yet. What will the future 'victim" be? Will there ever be an end to madness? As long as money and power can be gained here, unfortunately, there is no end in sight.

So, why am I so contemptuous toward the anti-bully movement? Because it's ineffective and in fact creates *more* bullies. Those who are already doing the bullying find new ways to bully others through these programs and those who are the bullied end up bullies themselves. Rather than moving on, they fixate on what happened to them and let it eat at them. Does this sound a little dramatic? That's because it is, but that's how victims of bullies see things, but it's a picture that the Victim Culture encourages. If not for the intervention of the "well intended" the victims would be better off. Dr. Anne Peterson, a doctor in Adolescent Psychology found in her research, that "the majority of adolescents ... successfully negotiate this developmental period without any major psychological or emotional disorder, develop a positive sense of personal identity, and manage to forge adaptive peer relationships... [And] maintain close relationships with their families." All without the help of those enablers, how do they do it?

In the book, *Dear Bully*, known authors talk about their experiences with bullies the one of Tonya Hurley is the most telling: "I've dreamed about getting revenge on you more times than I can count. And if I ran into you on the street today, I would have two words to say. Thank You.

Your cruelty and insensitivity were a wake-up call, a lesson in life I would not have learned otherwise... You prepared me for the world... More than anything you motivated me ... [no] matter how hard I tried to block you out ... your criticism stuck with me ... making me doubt myself, ... persevere and succeed... See, without you, there would be no me, at least not the me I came to be."

CHAPTER FIVE

THAT'S SO GAY

The calls for victimhood in this country go back a long way with the original calls of Women's Suffrage and the Civil Rights movements starting in the 1800's, but the Gay Rights movement didn't start until the 1960's so it has a lot of lost ground to cover.

As with the race and gender issues there have been times they had a point as well as being extremely wrong. In this chapter I will cover the issues of gayness of America.

REGULATING NUPTIALS

One of the most divisive issues in America today is that of Gay Marriage, with the

Social Democrats and the Traditional Republicans going head to head. With neither side backing down, neutrality is all but impossible–or is it? Is there a possible middle ground that hasn't been talked about, since no one is actually talking? If the two groups would stop and listen there is, but both sides need to give a little on the issue.

Within the Republican Party there's a realization that they need to make: you can disagree with something morally and still not support a law prohibiting it. A prohibition isn't coherent with limited government and it *always* has negative consequences. In this case the consequences are that by instituting the government in the issue, they have been granted the right to act and act they have. If the GOP hadn't requested a law making Gay Marriage illegal then the government wouldn't have ad hoc authority to intervene in an even worse way, granting Special Gay Rights. More entitlements for another "victim" special interest group, all so the "small government" could protect their personal morality, by legislative action. What's wrong with this picture?

Let me make this clear for those who might think I'm really acting for the Homosexual Lobby, I have *absolutely nothing* to gain personally with the gay marriage bans overturned. I've only known a few gay people, and a select few I would view as friends. On the other hand, I don't care if people are gay either. It's not that I'm for or against gays, it's that I distrust government *that much*. With every morality law decried we lose more and more of this great country and slip further into an authoritarian dystopia. A place where the governed personal choices are decided by the government and in this case of our *own request*.

NUCLEAR FAMILY MELTDOWN

One of the greatest emotional arguments against gay marriage is whether they should be allowed to adopt children because they could turn the children gay. Problem is there's no evidence to support the claim. Being raised in a family with two dads or two moms won't mean the children will be gay, it just means they grew up in an unconventional home.

Some would argue that that will mean they are singled out by bullies and will have an extra hard life. Is that a bad thing? Not necessarily. As we all know, our bad experiences teach us more than our good ones, we learn who we are and become stronger better people. These children who are going to "suffer" the hardships of being different will become stronger —as long as they are treated as victims anyway.

That's only part of the problem with the argument. The children that ended up gay came from traditional, heterosexual parents as well as from gay parents. That's what anti-gay rights advocates forget to mention. This is all to make sure children don't "turn" gay, but the problem is people are going to be gay or straight based on unknown factors, that are at this time not fully understood. While there are some questions that need to be addressed in the LGBT community, whether or not they should be allowed to raise children should be based on the same criteria—if they would have a dangerous home for the child—not on their sexual preferences.

LET THEM NOT EAT CAKE

As divisive an issue as marriage equality has proven to be, the issue of assault on religious freedom has—in some cases, at least—been a source of solidarity. The Christian bakers who have been legally strong-armed into baking cakes for gay couples for their weddings is the best example of this. Along with Christians, the Muslims have bakers that have suffered this as well—tell a Muslim they have to bake a cake for a gay wedding—that's a *great* idea! Try it a few *more* times, the problem will have solved itself. With the debate continuing about the legality and morality about businesses being able to refuse service to whomever they choose. This has prompted a Christian activist to turn around and do the same thing, going to bakeries run by gays and requested they to make their wedding cakes, and gays declined. This, however, has not received the same level of anger. Time will tell but with so many adamant that this kind of discrimination is immoral, because they passed a law–in Indiana the Religious Freedom Restoration Act–to enforce it.

On that part maybe they have a point, and if they had kept the legal statute out of it, there would be even more supporters on the side of businesses right to refuse service. I disagree with the businesses actions about discriminating against gay couples or vice versa–not only ethically, but it's not the best move economically either–but I stand behind them in their right to do so. I don't stand behind the gay rights activists in this, because they were intentionally going out to cause trouble, and at least one of the businesses involved has decided not to reopen for fear of reprisal. Those on the side of gay marriage or against it, many found a divergent point in the hostilities towards the mom and pop bakeries held hostage by gay rights activists. If common ground can be found in this instance can it be found in the greater discussion of the matter?

DON'T GOPROUD, JUST GO

The most puzzling attitudes are those directed towards the GOProud group, the gay Republican activist organization. Yes, they get comments by the social democrats, such as Michael Musto of *Village Voice* saying they are "like Jewish Nazis, Black Klan members... Roaches who moonlight as exterminators" or Joe Jervis saying GOProud members are "gestapo bootlickers." But that's the enemy, what about the reception from their "friends?" Why the alignment with the GOP instead of the Libertarian Party is anyone's guess, but what is clear is the relationship is a tenuous one at times. A couple of years ago the group was trying to be a part of CPAC but was denied access to the event. No matter your feelings about gay rights, so easily dismissing a sector of your base is simply idiotic.

This unfortunately is common with the GOP, they alienate their fringe sectors and potential party members with questionable actions and remarks. The only demographic they could be more hostile to–that could make a major part of the core base (than the gay community) is the Hispanic community. Now I'm not saying the party should go out and start indorsing "special rights" for either demographic or stop their struggle against illegal immigrants, but a change of tactic and rhetoric *could go a long way*. With the hostility that the democrats put on the more conservative members of both these groups it would make a lot of sense to be more welcoming to them. For example, with Hispanics change the dialogue of "it's immoral for illegals to get a bunch of freebies for coming to this country" to "it's immoral for *anyone* to get a bunch of freebies in this country."

In regards to gay marriage, we can take a lesson from the LDS church– known commonly as the Mormons. With the tides turning towards gay marriages and it being forced on religions and lawsuits in the works for executing their rights to refuse to do so, the church no longer performs government endorsed unions. This has freed them of their previous objections to gay marriages and they now have changed their minds on other discriminatory laws as well. This is great! Everyone *can* consider this a win as long as the Victim Culture crowd is ignored and the government is left out of the equation.

THAT'S SWEET, OKAY, THAT'S ENOUGH, STOP IT!

One of the examples used by gay rights activists, that America is still a hostile place to live if you're gay was the comments about the Michael Sam embrace with his partner at the news of his acceptance into the St. Louis Rams. That's not what the problem was, okay, with *some* people it was–but it was *more* than that. It was more about the openness of affection that bothered people. I was on *that* list as well, I don't care how they celebrate after the cameras are done rolling but I don't want to see it, no matter what their sexual orientation. Let me reiterate, if it had been a player with a wife I would not have wanted to see that either. Homosexuality was not the issue here–but it was turned into the issue. Since then, Sam has been cut and cut again. But the issue has been turned into the fact that he was gay, without having the pertinent question being asked: maybe he just sucks as a football player? For a moment, a micro-second, could it be considered that maybe he was an inefficient player? Is that too much to ask? Unfortunately sports is not immune to such controversies, such as issues of race and now homosexuality.

PEDOPHILES ARE PEOPLE TOO

In a lot of ways when it comes to gays and their call for equal treatment, they have kind of a point. By the beginning of the nineteen hundreds, the women's suffrage and the civil rights movement had passed major hurdles towards authentic equality. They even had achieved their own amendments to avoid voter discrimination and could marry interracially. The gay movement didn't start until the 1960's and didn't receive such autonomy with marriage until the late nineties or early 2000's. There are some issues that the LGBT community has to address, however, in regards to the conduct that they try to sweep under the rug.

The greatest concern has to do with the large number of serial killers who are gay. If it were only a couple of bad apples that would be one thing, but throughout history there have been a link between homosexuality and excessive violence. Jeffery Dahmer was probably the most well-known example–he murdered and cannibalized sixteen known gay boys–and in the end it cost him his life, when he was killed by a fellow inmate because of it. The question not being asked: is being gay the reason, or did it simply make them more opportune victims? Serial killers target the outsiders: the homeless, prostitutes and, yes, homosexuals. Could *that* be the real reason for the violence within the gay community? Or is there are a genetic link towards violence in gay men? Maybe an environmental one? With the hostility of simply posing such questions, we might never find out.

IT'S A LIFESTYLE CHOICE NOT A P.R. STUNT

Probably the most disturbing aspects within the gay culture is their rampant adulation of anybody who comes out as gay, not because it's a bad a thing to be supportive of others in making a hard admission–but because of the opportunities for exploitation by those who can profit from it. Look at the list of those who have suspiciously gained notoriety after "coming out"–Rosie O'Donnell, Ellen DeGeneres, and Michael Sam all have profited from their announcements. Is this ever cause for concern in the LGBT community? Have they ever wondered if they came out to help themselves more than the culture? I haven't heard it. I'm not saying they aren't genuine or they don't care about the future of their lifestyles, but isn't it a little disgusting how they seem to have used it to further their careers?

Then we have someone who refused to whore herself as a lesbian to advance her career. She's not only gay, and a woman, but a *black* gay woman, and she still doesn't want that to define her. She is Raven Symone, a former child star who as an adult has chosen to be reclusive and less in the spotlight. She still has enough pull to be an Oprah and that is where she stated that she isn't a gay person or black person, but a "human being." If only more thought this way and cared more about the human race than their particular place in it.

HOMOSEXUAL SAPIEN

To be fair to the anti-gay rights activists the LGBT community and its supporters have not always acted reasonable either. Forcing religious people to make cakes for their unions, ignoring the links between serial killers and homosexuality, and pushing around anyone who disagreed with them rather than trying to create an open dialogue. *Both* sides have been wrong. Another tack that *might not* be in the best interest of the gay community is the "we were born this way" argument. That might be so, but it's an unnecessarily polarizing declaration. It makes it sound like there are two different species here, not gay and gay. There is already enough division at the hands of the enablers of victim culture and identity politics that we don't need the "victims" themselves to make things any worse.

CHAPTER SIX

THE WORLD'S FLAT AND OTHER EPIC ENVIRONMENTAL FALLACIES

We've been taught in school that one of the reasons for the skepticism of Columbus' trail to the New World was that the world was believed to be flat. Truth is the world was never considered flat, this was literary license by the author of the earliest autobiography of Christopher Columbus. For years this piece of literary fiction was considered authentic truth, but this is not the only piece of fiction that has not properly analyzed and reviewed–most of the Climate

Change argument is this way.

Personally, I don't care if people put stock in the green movement but the problem is that they push for action when the evidence of "Man-Made" Climate Change is still so inconclusive. We have over 31,000 scientists–a substantial leap from the 700– that signed a statement saying it's not true. One of the founders of Green Peace, says the green movement has lost not only their way but their senses, as well. Many have relied on such faulty logic and evidence in animal rights cases as well, linking the two together without anything to link. The greatest missing link it appears is the evidence for man's guilt in regards to the environment.

IN THE NAME OF PRAIRIE DOG

Have you ever read the list of endangered species? The list of endangered species is really *damn* long, with thousands of animals, including multiple species of coral, as well as insects and rodents. Reading it is excruciating! So thankfully for you, I've saved you the trouble. The most famous are the polar bear, panda and tiger, with data that is questionable to say the least. Their numbers are difficult to substantiate as is the information about the devastation to their homeland. That's not what I'm going to go into in this segment though, instead, there's the questionable status of the prairie dog to the list. Why is the prairie dog on the list? This rodent's population isn't in major decline–so what kind of idiocy would prompt it to be placed on the list? I's because its drop in numbers could affect another animal's outcome, the black-footed ferret. This rodent–which even *having* a rodent on the list, since they can so easy propagate is absurd–but to have an animal on the list *because it's a food staple of another* animal is a whole new level of "special."

The real problem of this comes with the outcome of this measure. The prairie dog, like every rodent, has large numbers and cause a large amount of damage to peoples' food crops. With its protected status, it means that farmers can't take the needed steps to protect themselves from the loss caused by the rodent.

MORE WORRIED ABOUT iWORRY

"An elephant is killed every 15 minutes," that's the war-cry to action by the activists at iWorry, a program set up by the David Sheldrick Wildlife Trust, a charity based in Kenya. According to the Trusts' own, Dr. Dame Daphne Sheldrick, the elephant could be extinct in the wild in about 12 years. Reportedly last year 36,000 African elephants were killed for their ivory "buying ivory only serves to fuel a trade which results in more senseless deaths of these beautiful animals. We can't let man-made extinction be the end of this iconic species," she continued. Their webpage is not dissimilar to the Humane Society's format complete with an "adopt an elephant" feature.

On October 4, 2014, the group even held an "International March for Elephants" boasting more than 18,000 participants taking to the streets to petition their government to establish a total moratorium of ivory in their country. Amongst the supporters of this cause is actress, Kristin Davis, from the *Sex and the City* franchise. "All elephants are under siege," said Davis." Elephants have such personality." That's one point Davis and I agree "elephants do have a lot of personality"–but it's not necessarily a pleasant one! Elephants are one of the most ill-tempered and destructive species on the planet, after Alec Baldwin. Unlike Davis, however, I'm not so eager to foist over control of a trade to any single group or the government–not without finding out the specifics of their course of action and examining all options.

All that is reported by the Sheldrick Trust is they call for an establishment for a "complete ban" internationally on ivory and to have the elephant wholly protected. Is that all? While the endeavor is a good one the results are not, as is common with activists leading with their emotions–going full steam ahead; without letting something like facts get in the way of their grand standing. Don't get me wrong, I don't want to see the extinction of the elephant (or any species for that matter). I think the world is worse off without the Tasmanian wolf, Dodo bird and Passenger Pigeon, but careful forethought of the best way to proceed is the only way to succeed. The game plan the Sheldrick Trust is pushing for has been tried numerous times without success, an ivory prohibition would be as successful as every other prohibition has been, but in this case it will end with the extinction of the elephant. The problem that is not being addressed: There's a lot of money involved here, and that won't end simply because you want it to.

As far-fetched as it might sound the only plan that will work isn't to increase restrictions on the ivory market but instead to lift the bans. Set up a legal market for ivory, then you will create a vested interest by a group to protect the species. Davis is obviously a caring individual (if you're an elephant at least, I don't know how she is with people), but caring doesn't get the job done if you ignore logic. What has any government done to successfully protect a species from demise? It was the Australian government that ignored the decreasing numbers of the Tasmanian Wolf, to protect the sheep trade; it was the laws of the United States government that killed the orphan fawn "Giggles" in Wisconsin; it was the government that turned a blind eye at the numerous needless killings of peoples' dogs by overzealous policemen; and it was the government that took away a man's pet raccoon, simply because they could. The way to that save the animals from extinction are through the individuals; the people of the Sheldrick Trust, Kristin Davis, the zoos and other establishments. People who care enough to step in and do something—not callous and ignorant governments, that's the same with human activities, they only make things far worse.

REVENGE FOR CLARENCE DARROW

In the realm of animal rights activism we have reached a whole new level of bizarre–animals can now *sue* you. Extremist lawyers and activists have found a new cash cow and that's no longer just an expression! If you mistreat an animal, according to the vague definition given by activists, you could lose everything to *your own pet.* How can an animal actually sue you when they don't know what the legal system even is? A lot of people don't either, so I guess that's a tad redundant on my part. With the absurdity that has perforated the legal system in the last few years, because of Victim Culture, maybe this is simply the natural evolution of things. Monkey see, monkey sue.

DOWN WIND TO CANCER

With the death of John Wayne the

country, no the world, lost one of its most talented and gentlemanly human beings ever born. A humble man who spoke gruffly; but it being only the truth that some didn't want to hear. While the movie *True Grit*–for which he received a long overdue Academy Award–might not have been his best film; its title alone was fitting to the man who brought the character of "Rooster Cogburn" to life. John Wayne–The Duke–lived a *True Grit* style of life. The greatest tragedy was the manner his death was manipulated.

Wayne's film, the *Conqueror*, wasn't his trademark Western, but that of a portrait of Genghis Khan, filmed at the Snow Canyon National Park in Utah–a state common for films, because of the area's picturesque landscape. Where a few miles away in the Nevada desert, the federal government was conducting atomic testing detonating atomic bombs for study. Those tests provided us with a lot of valuable data about the effects of nuclear radiation that we might not have discovered otherwise. Unfortunately, a part of that knowledge was just how devastating it could be from a distance. During the filming of Wayne's movie the winds sent radiated dust particles from the "fallout" site over the cast and crew. Members of the cast died of cancer, the "Duke" was among them. The biggest problem with that conclusion is that Wayne was a big drinker and smoker, the "down-winder" theory in his case ignores that fact.

It's hard to say whether Wayne died from radiation induced cancer or from his personal vices, but it's not unreasonable to assume that was the major trigger of the cancer in the cast of the film. This, however, is only the beginning of the story and not the ending. To this very day people still use the "Duke" to try and cash in as victims–or the relatives of– "down-winders." Their claims have been checked out for authenticity of their merits, a study of the soil in the region was evaluated for radiation. To be fair it was elevated, but it wasn't the top layer and radiation's source couldn't be proven. The "down-winders" are adamant that they are owed for those tests and as with the other "victims" it wouldn't matter how explosive the evidence against their claims were, to them they will always be right.

PROTECTING A GIANT HOLE IN THE GROUND

The green movement is actually a lot older than most of us realized, with accounts from Aristotle and other philosophers. One of the earliest American attempts at reining in our industry was when President Theodore Roosevelt set up the national parks through executive action. He argued that since the landmarks were treasures that need to be preserved, that federal intervention was appropriate and the only way to protect against development. That's why we have a monument to the giant hole in the ground, the Grand Canyon. I know what you're thinking. It was Roosevelt's predecessor, Woodrow Wilson, who signed the National Parks Act in 1915 but it was Roosevelt that instituted the presidential precedent.

A fitting statement to how government works: throw money into a hole in the ground and hope for the best! The greatest inquiry I have with all this: Is the stated justification for protecting these natural landmarks the real reason for the law or is there one of less well intention? For instance: what is in the ground in the sanctioned deserts of the southwest? Oil pockets? Coal reserves? Or maybe a few veins of silver or gold. Whatever the perceived *need* for such legislature, the outcomes of it is far less obscure and have proven burdensome.

CENSORING CONTENTION

On the issue of progressive cowardice, the environment is the strongest example. They don't want there to be the slightest bit of contrary opinions out for further consideration. With the calls for such extreme actions to resolve climate change, it's disturbing to see emails stating "the fact is that we can't account for the lack of warming at the moment," or "I think we have to stop considering 'Climate Research' as a legitimate peer-reviewed journal." The authors of these messages have erased them, so finding them for further inquiry is impossible. More cowardice!

Another anonymous message read, the "next time I see [climatologist, Pat Michaels] ... I'll... beat the crap out of him." Pat Michaels is one of the more skeptical in the scientific community when it comes to man-made global warming, and we can't possibly have anyone asking questions! Be careful or you'll be sleeping with the fishes.

If these comments are from our social academics that is simply unacceptable–not only for the vitriol towards their skeptical peers, but because of the anger *towards their descent*. They are not saying that man isn't responsible for the climate shift, they simply are asking for sound data to show by how much. For their trouble they get threats of violence! The very purpose of science is to conduct inquiry free from bias, clearly that is missing here. As it is when Geographer Richard Glover says "surely it's time for the climate-change deniers to have their opinions *forcibly* tattooed on their bodies" [emphasis added]. Hope you got a lot of ink.

EVEN NASA CAN'T AGREE

One day I came across an interesting YouTube video that was put out by a NASA scientist and adamant supporter of the Climate Change movement. In the video, he showed the circulating air currents using thermal imagery to highlight the hotter temperatures. The footage did show increased temperatures, that was proven, but what happened later was more compelling. Those hotter temperatures were only during part of the year but ended up dissipating as the year went on. Not a very convenient fact for the green movement, also not convenient is that NASA is not in solidarity with

Climate Change. A couple of the most devout skeptics of mankind's unintentional decimation of our ecosystem are NASA scientists. Other skeptics are from other government agencies formed because they dared to challenge this dogma.

WATCH OUT FOR COW FARTS

The ridiculousness in the green/animal rights movement couldn't be made clearer; than when they ran with the joke made up by its detractors. When the discussion of dangerous particulate emissions comes up, a "denier"–such as myself–might point out, that a cow passing gas creates more methane than the cars on the highway. This wound up being a bad idea. It ended up playing into the dialogue of the green agenda. So how dangerous is a cow fart? How exactly do we test and quantify that? Well, I'm sure it will end up costing a lot of money and we'll not find out the answer.

It just goes to show that you can't make a

green joke around a social democrat, it goes over their heads.

OCD ABOUT CCD

Ever hear of Colony Collapse Disorder? It's a real thing and a real danger, or so it's claimed to be at any rate. Basically, the bees are in trouble and as always we are the culprit. According to the theory, our usage of certain pesticides are causing health issues for the bee's immune systems in some species. So of course, the chemicals responsible must be outlawed even though this is still speculative at this point. Didn't learn anything from what happened with DDT, I see. For those unfamiliar with DDT, it was an insecticide that was outlawed because it was deemed responsible for the thinning of eggshells in regional birds, but that was never conclusively proven–they banned it anyways! The replacement solutions haven't worked and they had bring back DDT. As with most examples of our impact on the planet, this too is being advanced with little evidence to support it; for the most part the "experts" don't even bother looking for proof, but assume that it must be because of mankind. To be fair it could be because of a different action by man, the introduction of the Africanized "Killer" bees into the continent. These hyper-aggressive species of bees don't play well with others, their docile cousins could be in that mix. Have the experts looked into it? Probably not.

The other point they make with this is the impact of the loss of the bees that will be detrimental to all animals because there won't be any other beings to pollinate our plants and we will lose all our crops. So, what happened to the other insects, or hummingbirds, or bats?–They also pollinate the plants as well. Even if all these creatures did go extinct, what makes the experts think that something else won't come along and fill the niche? They believe in evolution and *isn't that the basic idea behind evolution?* Won't the superior species just take that job?

EVOLUTION'S A LIE?

I have a lot of respect for Scott Walker, he showed real guts and determination when he took on the unions in his state, then he did something far less admirable–he made a statement saying that he doubts evolution. Not a good idea. One of the biggest stereotypical views of republicans is that they are "anti-science" and with the ones like Walker, who do have a brain (unlike, the agitators Mike Huckabee and Rick Santorum) it's obvious the detractors have a point. To Walker's credit, evolution doesn't prove everything all the time, but saying that it's wrong because of that? That doesn't do anything but stir up a hornet's nest!

Atheist scientists can be downright mean to those who doubt evolution, which is why creative design proponents justify their taking every opportunity to prove them wrong. Is this really how Christens are supposed to behave? I thought it was customary to "turn the other cheek?" Besides an obvious disconnect with their theological principles, is an eagerness to ignore evidence. That *is* anti-scientific. In fact, it seems downright reminiscent of the archaic mentality of those who imprisoned Galileo. I don't have a problem with anyone believing whatever–as long as they don't justify violence in the name of their theology, or scam people with it–but I do have a problem with them using it to advance hostility towards others. At least Walker didn't do that in the process, maybe Huckabee and Santorum could learn a thing or two.

VEGETABLE GENOCIDE

If you really consider it, the collusion between animal rights activists and the environmental movement is actually odd, if not completely paradoxical. Think about it, the green movement is about saving the trees and the animal rights crowd is about eating them instead of steak. Some of the rhetoric from the animal rights crowd is downright dumb really. They claim that since it doesn't have active intelligence or play, then a plant is not a living thing and that makes it appropriate to eat. But a plant is a living thing, so this still goes counter to their mantra. So, what can the anti-meat extremists eat? How about dirt? No, same problem, there are lifeforms in dirt too. More than that commercially made "dirt" usually has dangerous fertilizers and other additives making it unsafe for human consumption. They could go on a water diet, I guess, but I doubt they would last very long. Besides, if that was the case the radicals would declare a drought and make water difficult–if not almost impossible–to get. Like in California! The human body can sustain itself on water, just not for long. After a while it will need something more.

Between the excessive regulations, the hypocrisy, the mess of our legal system due to zealots like PETA, and using the memory of the Duke, the environmental victims have a lot to answer for.

CHAPTER SEVEN

WARNING: HISTORICAL CONTENT

History is written by the winners

of the struggles, not by those who end up in the hangman's noose. Sometimes sorting out the truth among the lies can be the greatest challenge in telling an historical tale. When it comes to the Victim Culture this is definitely no exception. This is not a history book though, it is philosophical text and the context of whether these stories are true or not, are less important than the fact that they are becoming common and what they mean to the culture by and large.

REAL INDIAN TAKERS

In the name of reparations the Native Americans want their piece of the pie. Because of the conduct of the United States representatives of the past–the Trail of Tears, under the administration of Andrew Jackson for one–claims that we, the American people should take care of them. This disturbing trend is a far cry from the sentiments of a "once proud people." Is this really the descendants of the proud warriors who took on the encroaching federal government? Are their new greatest ambitions, living on food stamps and living in the ramshackle government housing? It doesn't matter where government housing is set up, if it's the reservations or the ghettoes of Harlem, the government assistance takers end up as victims– victims of government serfdom.

SLAVES OF ALL SHADES

It's entertaining to hear black racial activists talk about slavery– they make it sound like they have the exclusive monopoly on slavery and its emotional distress. The way they talk, you would think that slavery didn't happen to any other group and that it starts in America. Even in America, the blacks aren't alone when it comes to slavery. It began with the Native tribes by the Spaniards; and the Mexican and Chinese being enslaved during the building of the railroads. But slavery didn't start here in the US either. It was a well-established tradition across the planet, long before the Declaration of Independence was even written. The primitive tribes–in basically every nation–have held their "inferiors" as captives for their bidding.

The African tribes would sell off captured members of a different tribe to the Europeans for the slave trade, or keep them for their slaves or sacrifices. Why are they never mentioned in the subject of subjection? Same with the Central American and South American tribes. For millennia, Jews have been used as slaves–by many different cultures—such as the Egyptians and the Third Reich. Even whites have not been immune to the scourge of slavery, with the Irish and Scottish clans as indentured servants to the British.

DECONSTRUCTING THE ALAMO

It's not only the descendants of black slaves and the Native Americans that think modern Americans "owe" reparations, the Mexicans need to get in on the racket as well. The claim is that since Americans fought for and captured land that was once part of Mexico, we have wronged them and they want that land back. Historically speaking, if you go by that standard then they probably owe reparation to other tribes too, since the Latin tribes were warriors who took from other tribes or maybe from a Native American tribe. If that's the case are *they* going to give it back? Since the tribe they took it from is most likely long since extinct that would be rather difficult. Actually, most tribes *including* the Mexica tribe that was part of the Aztlan tribe, they adamantly claim as their predecessors, have gone extinct–according to experts. If this is true then they have *no* claim to the Southwest and are, in all likelihood, the descendants of the Spanish who ravaged the ancient Latin tribes.

Let's put all that aside for a moment and say they are right. The land was part of Mexico and should go back to it. Why would they want to do that? Look at what their leaders do with the land they have, if they have more will they suddenly be more humane and benevolent to their people? Highly unlikely, since that offers no incentive to do so. In fact they might even double down on their oppression from the emotional high given from the land expansion. There has been a change in a positive direction in Mexico in the recent past, with the booting of President Fox. Their new president is trying to get rid of the cartels and increase manufacturing in their infrastructure. As a nation they are starting to explore for natural resources, creating more jobs there, but they are still openly hostile towards the US; claiming we're racist for wanting to keep Mexicans in Mexico. In Mexico there's a mixed bag of restrained optimism and brutal reality at their prospect of getting out of the victims industry.

THINK OF THE CHILDREN

One of the biggest cultural lies, has to be the reasons for child labor laws. We have been lead to believe they were created to protect the children. Not even close! They were created to protect union jobs, they couldn't care less about the children, and if they did these laws wouldn't have been implemented. Besides the fact that the children enjoyed contributing, at times it was a necessity for the family in hard times. Many families wouldn't have made it, or would have had to turn to the government for assistance—during the great depression, for example—if not for their children pitching in. Self-reliance, we can't have that! So, under the guise of "protecting the children", the government killed two birds with one stone: get more people hooked on federal money and pay back the unions. The children and their families–who were supposed to be protected really did end up victims.

AMELIA EARHART'S REAL CONTRIBUTION

Everyone knows Amelia Earhart for her aviation career and the infamous lost flight, but that wasn't what her real legacy was–it was in the body politic, especially in the realm of abolition and feminism. She petitioned–along with other feminists–for the passage of the odious Equal Rights Amendment (ERA). ERA was advanced by Lucretia Mott and written by Alice Paul of the National Women's Party, of which Earhart was a huge supporter. As with feminists now, not all were really interested with equality and leveling the playing field as much as fostering contention and clouding the facts behind what was really going on. Unlike the race relations pioneer Booker T. Washington (covered in a later chapter), Earhart didn't advocate women building themselves up, as much as tearing gown the social institutional structures and taking from men. She didn't really advocate creating much at all–seeing as she was a supporter of the early forms of birth control and a critic of marriage, marrying more out of social custom than anything.

During the 2012 presidential campaign, Anne Romney received a lot of flak from the feminist movement because of her pro-family and pro-marriage comments, chiding her because she was content with her role as a wife and mother and not wanting to pursue a career. Feminist Hillary Rosen commented, "This isn't about whether Ann Romney or I or other women of some means can afford to make a choice and stay home and raise the kids. Most women in America, let's face it, don't have that choice. They have to be working moms and home moms. And that's not the piece I am hearing from the Romney camp." Michelle Malkin had this to say about the comments from feminists, "We're damned if we do stay home and we're damned if we don't. We're damned because we conservative women drive the Left and its feminist shills mad with our fierce belief in protecting our families from the Nanny State, our embrace of free-market principles, and our rejection of the perpetual victim/grievance mentality."

Actress Kaley Cuoco, star of the series *8 Simple Rules For Dating My Daughter* and *The Big Bang Theory*, had similar sentiments and also was criticized. This is the feminist movement in action, a movement that has no clear ethics behind achieving their demands and in the end is nothing more than propaganda–the same notion of "equality" being forced on us today.

BILLY GOT A BAD RAP

In my book *UNConventional Wisdom* I talk about a theory of mine, referred to as "Magnet Theory", in which the forces of government and crime are either in alignment or opposition, With the illegal and immoral actions during the era of the Great Depression and Prohibition, the incentives for the mob was to act in a manner to gain favor with the people. If not for the St. Valentine's Day Massacre the tide of public sentiment might have stayed with the mob.

This theory is not only observable to that time period, but to early time periods and the modern era, as well. Take for example the life of Billy the Kid, even now there is much debate on whether "the kid" was justified in his original intent during the Lincoln County War. After his employer was murdered the corrupt cattle ranchers and the law–in league with the cattle barons– wouldn't do anything, Billy and the other employees of John Tunstall went after his killers. It should be mentioned that Billy was deputized at this time and enlisted to serve warrants for the known perpetrators, but his anger got the best of him. Instead of simply going after the killers he decided to *take on the system that killed Tunstall.* He shot the sheriff and other that were in cahoots with the cattle monopoly and went down in history as a blood-thirsty killer himself, but note that records showed he only killed five men and not twenty. To maintain perspective, keep in mind the attitudes of his time and place. In this context his actions are not even really unusual as far as the lack of respect for human life. What had earned him the bad reputation wasn't the body count but who he had shot.

ON TO THE EARPS

While Billy the Kid's celebrity is that of an outlaw and cold-blooded killer, the famous law man, Wyatt Earp, has the reputation of a tough-but-honorable officer of the peace. In a lot of ways he was and all he was doing was following the letter of the law, but what if the law was wrong, like Billy the Kid thought? In many towns of the old west, guns were not allowed in town and just like we see today that has caused problems. Namely the same problem, those who need a tool of self-defense follow the law and are victimized; those who wish to cause trouble, simply ignore the law and carry guns in town.

Even though I don't condone Billy the Kid's actions, he was on to the crux of the problem–the law enforcers don't always enforce the law, but create its own to justify their violations of the public. The notorious Cowboys, (the group of outlaws terrifying the townspeople of Tombstone where the OK Corral was located) were criminals, but they had the legal protection to carry guns where ever they wanted. That is what the second amendment grants to all, the right of self-preservation in whatever form we feel most comfortable. It was the illegal confiscation of the Cowboys' firearms that was the cause of the OK Corral shootout, Earp was enforcing an illegal law. He had to maintain law and order and the Cowboys had a habit for disrupting that, but in the OK Corral the Earps were wrong.

THE TRUTH BEHIND TRUTH

Another icon of the feminist movement who shouldn't be is the activist Sojourner Truth. Born Isabella Baumfree, she was the daughter of slaves and one herself at the end during the abolition movement. She ended up getting passed around from one slave master to another, sold with a flock of sheep for $100 to John Nelly that Truth recounts as being a violent and harsh man.

She ended up being sold a couple more times until ending up with John Dumont, where she learned to speak English. During her time at the Dumont residence, she fell in love with a slave named Robert from the neighboring farm, and they had a daughter. Robert's owner forbade their relationship because any other children would be Dumont's property. Dumont compelled a union for Truth with another slave, Thomas, and they married and had two daughters and a son. As emancipation was looming for Truth and her family, John Dumont reneged on his promise to free her and she "did not run away, I walked away by daylight." She learned that her son had been sold to an Alabama man and she took him to court and won, setting a precedent as the first successful challenge of a black woman against a white man.

After her emancipation, Truth converted to Christianity, which she used as her platform against slavery and civil rights. She joined an activist gathering in Northampton, Massachusetts; the Northampton Association of Education and Industry, where she met other famous abolitionists such as William Lloyd Garrison, Frederick Douglass and David Ruggles. Truth was a radical amongst radicals, seeking political equality for women and demanding the black community include black women as well as men in their civil rights agenda. Even after the Emancipation Proclamation was decried, Truth still pushed for more– including property rights from land grants for former slaves. The causes that Truth fought for were right, her methods were not– she had that impatience that is so common amongst progressive activists and ultimately it causes problems. When you push too hard against the mountain of societal norms, you might create an avalanche, endangering yourself, your supporters and your cause. Especially when you deliver such a charged speech as this one:

> "Well, children, where there is so much racket there must be something out of kilter. I think that 'twixt the negroes of the South and the women at the North, all talking about rights, the white men will be in a fix pretty soon. But what's this here talking about?
>
> That man over there says that women need to be helped into

carriages, and lifted over ditches, and to have the best place everywhere. Nobody ever helps me into carriages, or over mud-puddles, or gives me any best place! Ain't I a woman? Look at me! Look at my arm! I have ploughed and planted, and gathered into barns, and no man could head me! And ain't I a woman? I could work as much and eat as much as a man–when I could get it–and bear the lash as well! And ain't I a woman? I have borne thirteen children, and seen most all sold off to slavery, and when I cried out with my mother's grief, none but Jesus heard me! And ain't I a woman?

Then they talk about this thing in the head; what's this they call it? [member of audience whispers, "intellect"] That's it, honey. What's that got to do with women's rights or negroes' rights? If my cup won't hold but a pint, and yours holds a quart, wouldn't you be mean not to let me have my little half measure full?

Then that little man in black there, he says women can't have as much rights as men, 'cause Christ wasn't a woman! Where did your Christ come from? Where did your Christ come from? From God and a woman! Man had nothing to do with Him.

If the first woman God ever made was strong enough to turn the world upside down all alone, these women together ought to be able to turn it back, and get it right side up again! And now they is asking to do it, the men better let them.

Obliged to you for hearing me, and now old Sojourner ain't got nothing more to say."

I think "old Sojourner" said plenty!

CRUCIFYING COLUMBUS

Many people end up looking like the bad guy when a review of history takes place. Someone who has suffered most is

Christopher Columbus. To be fair, Columbus was a horrible human being, he enslaved and killed many of the Native American tribes and stole a lot of their national riches. Being a human rights titan is not what he's remembered for though; he's remembered for his contributions as an explorer. Should his conduct really be so readily dismissed because of this? This is after all, based on the views of race at the time after all, not on ours. Which accordingly, he would be in line with the common consensus in European exceptionalism.

There are a lot of myths surrounding not only Columbus, but the view of the world around him. The sad thing is Columbus is the one who is being punished here, having his name attached to slavery, racism and genocide is not inappropriate, but ignoring that it was the common attitude of his era is. The Europeans didn't have a problem with slavery and also saw the Native Americans and Negroes and slaves. But remember so did the other tribes as well. Why are they never questioned about this? The simple answer–if you can consider it that–it doesn't play into the "white guilt" narrative.

INDIGENOUS PEOPLE DAY PARADE

With the condemnation of Columbus in full swing the progressive end result has become clear–abolish Columbus, which in turn means they can abolish everything he stands for. The United States is an amazing place, full of millions of different opinions and cultures, we are a multicultural melting pot and always have been and should stay that way.

Many people–in the name of addressing tolerance, mind you–want to change that and want only their voices heard. This is beyond sad. Part of being tolerant is hearing out those we disagree with and understanding that maybe they have some valid points or concerns. When climate change is brought up, and severe interventions are proposed to curtail it, there should be an open dialogue about the consequences of these measures—which includes asking, how is man really affecting the planet? But that is not what is being done, the progressive way to fix this is to silence the critics. When people question how effective common core is, they should be given their chance to make their case too. Unions, under the guise of protecting the children, claim that asking how well a teacher performs will be detrimental to their child. What really harms a child is *not* properly vetting our educators and the environment in which that they receive their tutelage. The issues of gay rights and abortion, cause discussion to break down as well. As does illegal immigration; both sides have extreme solutions to fix it, of which neither make much sense. But I listen and continue to offer up my solutions to these issues.

These are all far more complex than most want to think they are and each side sees only their side of it. Not always because they are lazy, some people are, but also because smart people become stubborn. Stubbornness that is fueled by emotional attachment to the issue. That is more of a reason to encourage an honest debate, not abandon it. If not, we will end up with the Indigenous Peoples Day Parade and other politically correct holidays, free from the burden of contentious tolerance.

HOW ATHIESTS CAN STILL LOVE JESUS

As I'm sure you've noticed, I have very little respect for anchor Bill O'Reilly, he's a loud-mouth, obnoxious pontificator, who doesn't care about others opinions. In fairness, I do have to commend him on his *Killing* series. The only one that I have read is *Killing Kennedy*, but it was an amazing book, the rest I saw on National Geographic after they adapted them for TV presentations. The one I want to focus on in this segment is *Killing Jesus*. O'Reilly got a lot of unfair criticism for this book and it was mostly from religious people, the most common criticism being that it was not more of a religious text. It wasn't supposed to be, it was supposed to be based exclusively on the historical text.

When I was watching it something dawned on me, that the story of Jesus could still be appreciated by those who don't believe in him. He was pretty tough actually, with his not giving in to the Jewish heads of state and the Romans. From a political standard he would be a libertarian, because he hated the sin and loved the sinner, neither the republican or democratic parties do that. Sure, they don't call for stoning people, but that wanted to imprison people for minor legal infractions–with laws based on personal standards. He took on the Roman and Jewish authorities face on and exposed the theocracy and corruption in the area. In doing so, he exposed the vulnerability of the Roman authoritarians and that personal choices should be made by the person and not the state. Anyone who believes that can look up to Jesus, even if *some* of those who follow him act inappropriately or contrary to what He taught.

CHAPTER EIGHT

FOR THE LOVE OF MONEY

There's a direct correlation between the claims of racism and victimhood culture, and anti-capitialist sentiments. Whether it's White Privilege, lawsuit abuse, feelings about non-profits, pawn shops and Walmart, and the collected consensus on money itself. For the most part it's lead by unions, special interests groups and other Marxist and socialist constructs.

WHITE PRIVILEGE: WHAT AM I DOING WRONG

I can't help but laugh when I hear

comments of White Privilege come from racial instigators. White Privilege? What White Privilege? I've had to work hard to earn every promotion, and I had to make sacrifices for my business. If that sounds like an unfair advantage in my favor you're insane. I've never gotten a thing because I'm white, but many have a lot of unearned money and privileges by claiming that I have White Privilege.

With Affirmative Action and other such laws, that give others special treatment no one is treated fairly. Those who are passed up for an earned promotion because they are white or male, to fill some absurd quota is the most obvious victim, but those who get the unearned promotion are a victim as well. They lose the opportunity to better themselves. They become the victim of a scheming politician who would have complacent masses rather than a thinking and hard-working one.

So, here's my challenge for anyone who believes socialism is a good thing. Before you trash capitalism, try it. Try setting up your own business, try the 60-80 hour weeks, the cutting through the financial and zoning paperwork, building something with your own blood, sweat and tears. If you try, you will understand the unbelievable high that you get from making your own mark.

COMPLETELY SUED

Every time I see an ad on T.V. for these class action lawsuits it makes me cringe. Do you have Mesothelioma? Do you have a malfunctioning vaginal mesh? Do you have an artificial hip that's not working properly? Have you or loved one died from any of these? I'm curious if anyone has made that phone call–"Yes, I died from Mesothelioma and I'm looking for representation." You've got to admit that would be funny and the conmen attorneys' do deserve it.

Now, before you start thinking I'm heartless, let me explain my reason for distain with all this. To begin with, these ads are not *by* attorneys but a "non-attorney spokesman." Okay, what the hell does that even mean? Well, for starters, it means this has nothing to do with the law and everything to do with money. It also means those involved with the ads are more than likely angry and looking to get even with the medical community because they had a loved one die. These are people who have turned the medical malpractice lawsuit into a career and it has had deadly ramifications for the healthcare field.

When medical professionals have to pay more due, to excessive lawsuits, they have to pass on the expense to their patients. If not, they would go out of business pretty quick. Another extra expense has to do with the expense of equipment due to the lawsuits; if they're lucky the equipment only goes up in price–many of them close up shop. The costs associated with lawsuit leaves us with less choices, hurts the doctor-patient relationship and has given rise to the government health care monopoly and all this was *before* the Affordable Care Act.

ROMANCING THE NON-PROFITS

We as a nation love our non-profits and from the perspective of the Social Democrats and other progressives it's easy to understand why, but from capitalists, this is a bit baffling really. The major reason it's confusing is that non-profits are a fairly anti-capitalist concept as a notion and in function. Think about it, this goes right in line with the Marxist concept of money being the "root of all evil" and non-profits get tax exempt status without the scrutiny of the taxpayer. That doesn't sound like very good policy to me.

To further demonstrate this, look at the sentiment toward the National Write Your Congress versus its NPO (non-profit organization) counterpart Open Congress. As entities both get certain tax benefits, but Open Congress gets more and has less public scrutiny. When examining National

Write Your Congress, I found a few people considered it a scam with very vague reasons. The only reason many gave was because you had to pay for their services while with Open Congress you didn't. That doesn't make them a scam, it makes them a *for profit* business. Besides, just because a business claims to be non-profit doesn't mean it really is, or that it's really a free service for that matter. A little hint, if it has .gov at the end of the webpage, you *already paid* for it with your taxes.

While there are very good non-profits, such as certain charities, there are many that are basically scams. Pretty much any set up by Al Sharpton are an excellent example. He used them to try to set up a tax dodging system and got caught, but since he's Obama's first homey he more than likely won't face prosecution anytime soon. This is the criminal nature that is inherent in many non-profits and it comes from the void of the profit seeking incentive. All animals act according to incentive–at times good incentives, at times bad–with non-profits their incentive is not a good one because they will keep tax exempt status even if they are an unscrupulous individual like Mr. Sharpton. If they had to compete in the market place where their conduct is reviewed by the consumer, instead of the government, they wouldn't last. Not only because such perverse incentives are a breeding ground of corruption, but because there's no incentive to improve your product or service.

PAWNING THE PAWN SHOPS

One industry that have been placed in the crosshairs of the "Obamanomics" system is the pawn shops. A plethora of new regulations have been introduced by the Obama administration on these local shops that indicate how the president *really* feels about the poor. Pawn shops have a bad reputation, but are pivotal for those in need. They offer the needed access to quick cash in times of hardship and access to goods at a lower price than retail. Either the president is tone-deaf to one of the most simple and basic economic necessity or he just doesn't care–and *I'm* considered heartless?

THE PASSION OF JAY Z

There are a lot of people who don't like rap music; with its racial and misogynistic terms and themes, violent imagery, its advocacy for the welfare state, and its use of words considered obscene in the common culture, it's easy to understand why. Some are equally appalled by the fixation on money and the hypocrisy of the use of the word "nigger" in the lyrics. So, do the naysayers have a point? Does rap music only perpetrate violence and racism, without any redeeming value? Take the "first couple" of the music world, Jay-Z and Beyoncé. They are a couple of the biggest Obama cheerleaders and encourage racial tensions, so how can I possibly have anything *good* to say about them?

It is difficult, but there is something that

Jay-Z has done that is of a benefit to society: he became a genuine success. Many rappers are not what they appear to be; they borrow boats, and lavish cars and mansions, for their music videos–it's a show. Others–such as Lil' Jon–didn't grow up in poverty; he grew up in a four level house, with a pool in a tranquil Southwestern, Atlanta neighborhood. His parents were both white collar professionals. "We weren't … broke…" stated manager and childhood friend, Rob McDowell in an *Entertainment Weekly* interview. "We had go-karts and lots of toys." Lil' Jon corroborates this, "After graduation I was just living in mom's basement, getting drunk and playing video games… and then going out to DJ parties at night." Yeah, sounds like he was really struggling! Lil' Jon is not alone in his deception, take Wu Tang Clan performer, Ol' Dirty Bastard (O.D.B.). "As O.D.B. he was comfortable spinning a public a public mythology … that he had grown up on welfare, or … not known his father," reads a

New York Times article about his death. Both turned out to be works of fiction–"our brother looked at things as selling records. So he dismissed whatever lies he told as just a way of getting publicity," explains his sister, Monique James.

This obsession with money isn't necessarily helpful, but it does give a sense of hope, that maybe they can get out of the ghettos. The thing is this trickery is not exactly a trade secret, but in the case of Jay-Z he at least can say that he did. This former drug-dealer, set out to start his own production company his own clothing line; and has shown–by example– that even in the worst places in the US *anyone* can succeed if they are willing to take the risk.

THE EVIL ACTS OF WALMART

Walmart has always been a target by the progressive left because of the company's "human rights violations" in regards to the minimum wage. They were paying lower wages so they could keep more people employed and offer the shoppers the lowest price. That is the model that is common in other discount retail chains, like Ross. Now the superstores have come up with a way to increase their employee wages and still maintain low prices, that's great. If you ask a progressive what I–a libertarian–would have said, they would claim I would condemn this. Not at all, what I do condemn is the bullying from the progressives and unions. Mostly because they are trying to score points off of the actions of the company.

If you look through history many of the social wrongs were going down before federal intervention. The discriminations against women and minorities were going down before EEOC laws, as was employee safety prior to OSHA, after laws were passed–these advancements stagnated. With the natural progression of people's changing attitudes towards others; more progress was made than through the progressive's legislative push. The fact that Walmart raised its wages has more to do with capitalism and less to do with national busybodies meddling.

WITHHOLDING EMPLOYMENT

I hate to agree with Angela Davis, but on one issue she is partially right. Angela Davis is a Black Panther and Communist, as well as an infamous race instigator still propagandizing today. Her most infamous rants are against the "Prison-Industrial Complex" and she is determined to shut down all prisons. Instead, the focus should be on education and rehabilitation I agree that we need prison reform and to have our laws–both state and federal–audited, but a complete abolition of prisons? No, that's a dumb idea. There are some people who should be locked up, it doesn't matter how much education or rehab Charles Manson gets; he is still a heartless killer. Of course, since he's white (and a racist) Davis would probably be fine with leaving him in there.

But increasing rehabilitation opportunities

for non-violent offenders is where Davis' criticism of our prison system is valid and there have been great strides in this already. In the past a prison record meant that your life was basically over when you were released. I get that having a felon for an employee isn't ideal, but with the hostile environment they receive after they served their debt to society, doesn't leave them with many options. In order to get a job, they would have to lie or worse, forge a false identity altogether. With time this attitude and others have softened; *despite*, not because of, the calls for action by Davis.

UNINTENDED HUMANITARIANISM

Most of us who support the free market will accept the criticism that it doesn't always fix every problem. There have been it's dark times as well, during the industrial revolution, for example, many workers needlessly lost their lives because the actions of the capitalists who employed them. The contentions, however, were spurred on by the labor unions who only make money if there is discontent between employers and employees.

They convinced the workers they had a right to more than what their employer offered, and imagine that, they believed them. But they were wrong, they weren't entitled to anything, not even their position. The job and all the benefits that come with it are the sole property of the employer, to offer to whomever they choose. Their offering you a job is an act of benevolence, they are acting in a humane way. But this is not the only way that those evil capitalists perform unintended good deeds, by providing us all with their goods and services they make our lives better. In making already existing products "more improved", we are given a product that might last longer; or, has a new feature; a better taste or smell; or is cheaper or safer. This happens because they are trying to make money and beat their competition to it. This is the wonder that is capitalism, with all its occasional inadequacies.

CHAPTER NINE

PROGRESSIVES NEED ENEMAS

O ne of the greatest enablers of

the Victim Culture is the Progressive elite. This is about them.

WHO CAIRS?

The nonprofit group CAIR was founded in 1994 as a supposed voice for harassed and alienated Muslims in America. The mission statement of CAIR is "enhance understanding of Islam, encourage dialogue, protect civil liberties, empower American Muslims, and build coalitions that promote justice and mutual understanding." With their literature echoing this sentiments CAIR believes the "active practice of Islam strengthens the social and religious fabric of our nation." Interesting ... a religion that offers celestial paradise for the slaughter of anyone that doesn't believe as they do and hasn't advanced beyond that position in thousands of years.

A religion that claims it's morally appropriate to practice Sharia law, which has dismemberment or death for minor transgressions, and treats women and homosexuals as punching bags will "strengthen the social and religious fabric of our nation." A religion that Bill Maher is nervous about because its followers want to "kill you." A religion that practices genital mutilation on women and beheads those who dare to speak out against it but is simply misunderstood?

To help combat this wave of "hate crimes" against Muslims in America, CAIR established "CAIR-NET" an email system to identify the bias against Muslim Americans.

Do you think this would be fair to mention the hate crimes *perpetrated by Muslims?* Think it caught the guy who beheaded his coworker because she wasn't a Muslim? How about the Tsarnaev brothers bombing in Boston? Do think CAIR condemned anything that I mentioned, or just brushed it off as hyperbole from an ardent Islamphobe? If such actions were done from a white based group, I would still condemn them, but with CAIR the only civil liberties worth protecting are believers of Islam and it's fine if they "kill you" if you even show a picture of Muhammad.

CLIVEN BUNDY DISTRACTION

If you want to see a libertarian cry, one pretty surefire way is to mention one name, Cliven Bundy. That hurts even thinking about it. The Cliven Bundy incident was an important one, because it brought to the national forefront the needed discussion about federally owned land. In the Southwest, much of the land has been taken hostage by the federal government and *finally* there was an actual discussion on the matter thanks to Bundy.

Bundy supposedly owed the government a couple million dollars in back taxes, an issue that was never really resolved because of comments made by Bundy. Just as the issue was reaching a fervor, the old man did something that ruined it all and went on TV and made some questionable statements that at least sounded racist. That was the end of the discussion. It's hard to say for sure, but the comments were not *supposed* to be racist. Keep in mind, Bundy is simply an old rancher, he would not be used to being grilled for syllable nor trained in political correctness. He would be used to speaking his mind, in his own way. He's not a trained orator, such as Obama or other politicians or journalists. We all know *they never make verbal errors!* But those who wanted to silence Bundy were more than willing to spread the words of Bundy, while the "57 states" or the "Corpse-men" Obama gaffs went unchecked by the sleeping media.

U.N. THOUGHT: PROTECTING YOU FROM YOU SINCE 1945

The United Nations is probably the most revered of organizations of the globalist progressives, because it is their pass to intervention into the lives of all. Like the National Bank being reborn into the Federal Reserve and the Fairness Doctrine into Net Neutrality, the United Nations is another example of the progressive attitude that a bad program never dies, it just gets a name. The dismantling of the League of Nations would be a travesty, after all, and the United Nations ends up being more fitting anyways, with the common abbreviation of the U.N.

This is more appropriate because of the implications that it offers to the subject it addresses. The U.N. Peacekeeping agenda, with their burdensome sanctions and empire building in countries hostile to their goals, doesn't create peace at all. The U.N. Gun

Rights goals protects the gun rights for criminals only. The U.N. Environmental agenda advocates more electric cars, ignoring the fact that to produce the battery for the car creates more greenhouse gases than the car would have if it were gas powered; and also sanctions subsidies for alternative energies with regulations for fossil fuels that are disconnected with reality. These kinds of policies push prices up while the rest of us wait for their "break-throughs" in the green energies market. The U.N. Economic agenda is probably the biggest joke of all, governments can't grow the economy. They only regulate it to death and apparently doing so at the small scale wasn't good enough so they had to expand their meddling. When it comes to the U.N. there is no other group more qualified for "un-thought"; they have definitely mastered the skill.

EDUCATION HOSTAGE

Our nation's comparatively recent

obsession with education has not helped with getting us out of the last recession. We are still in what is referred to as a "buyer's market", in which the employer has all the advantage, and those with higher educations need a job so badly that they will work more menial jobs. This hurts us all; not only those that need those entry-level jobs, but those in the higher professions and society itself. It causes harm to society because those without an education can't find those jobs and better their situation, ultimately ending up on unemployment, but the harm also is the greater contribution the trained professional could be doing. If they were out doing their true trade, they could be hiring others to assist them in their occupation or even growing out their own company providing many other jobs. This is the price we pay for economic intervention, the government creates tides that alter the environment for business, through tax-breaks or taxation. Neither really causes long term effects and both actions are morally wrong. Either actions kills competition and manipulates the market giving an artificial advantage to one company while keeping out others. What we need is to reform the tax system so that all such advantages are eliminated. If anyone is given a tax break it should be everyone, not a select few; but on that token excessive taxation makes problems too. If we didn't have this tax system, we wouldn't have this distortion.

That's not to say the education/labor system doesn't have other problems, it does. The President's solution to student loans is a bad solution to a problem that will exacerbate our welfare spending. It's based on the premise that we are all entitled to an education, which is adamantly wrong. We are no more entitled to education than we are to health-care, these are both goods and services. As we can see, our education system isn't perfect; the solutions to try and fix other problems have led to more problems. The rest has to do with our ever growing dependence on the diploma.

NET NEUTERED

With all the concern for internet security because of the hacking of Sony, to be more specific, the Obama administration has been pressured into action by progressive groups such as Openmedia and Demand Progress. The groups claim that Comcast and other greedy corporate entities have kept the internet in chains and need to be reined in. Apparently, from their perspective, only the federal government can save the day making Obama Superman? That's a scary thought! Obama as Superman would apologize for interfering with the criminal, and then assist him in blowing up the building. Is that *too* inflammatory? I thought I was allowed to make such comments in this country, but maybe I was wrong. With the fundamental misunderstanding of the role of government in our lives, our "Superman" Obama has been eagerly waiting to advance a law to curtail freedom of speech and in Net Neutrality extensions he would have it.

On February 26, the FCC reviewed its position in our lives. Tom Wheeler–the current head of the FCC agreed with the Obama administration that new restrictions and regulations are needed, that is basically, a reincarnation of the Fairness Doctrine. What are the implications of this? Well, nothing good, unless you're an Obama lapdog. When the Fairness Doctrine was in place during the Roosevelt administration, it nearly killed radio, because the general public was losing interest. They didn't want to hear the social democrats or progressives emotional preaching. The claim was that because the *results* weren't the same, his progressive policies must not be given equal treatment by the radio industry–it never occurred to him that maybe the public didn't *want* to hear it. This is what Obama believes is the case with the internet. The public loves him, so there must be something non-egalitarian in the internet, right? Sorry

"Superman", the internet is already open and free, it's just a lot of people don't agree with you.

The internet, under the new guidelines, would mean censorship and higher prices for all. Despite the promises made by the Obama administration or the FCC, there will be no distinctions between the small no-budget blogger and those who manage the large power house media organizations. The fees will be less, but those who weren't charged before, would be now. It's also a very unnecessary move, the free market already regulates it. Many internet organizations already offer free options for their sites with the fees for additional features. Some say this is unfair. That doesn't make sense, you should have to pay for extended services.

Freedom of speech is such a cherished and needed right, it is the pillar for a free society, something that we take for granted and others covet. Our nation has always been unique in that we have that freedom and our leaders have been looking for ways to curtail our speech when it becomes "inconvenient." Starting with John Adams, our second president, who wrote the sedition acts. Jailing journalists and pamphleteers for writing scathing editorials about Adams. During World War I, President Wilson brought these laws back, incarcerating critics of America's involvement in the war. Roosevelt also used such laws during World War II. That's why the criticism of the Vietnam War seemed so intense, it was *actually allowed!* Our freedom of speech is so valuable, that so many fought to the death for it and our most egotistical representatives fought–and continue to fight–to destroy it. The internet is the last refuge for such freedoms and worth fighting for, if we let the government neuter it we will regret it.

CHICAGOLAND

Probably the most backwards city in America is that of Chicago, even beating out Detroit–at least they have started making an effort to fix their situation. Chicago could learn from Detroit, but instead they insist on embracing the unions who in this case, have flamed the fires of racial animosity as well as anti-capitalist rhetoric. At the teacher unions rallies, the sentiments have been that Chicago is a "black's only city." Has this been addressed by any of the city officials? Of course–not! The leaders of the Democratic run city are fine with this, in fact some welcome it.

The only one in the "Party of the People" who has shown any discontentment with it is Rahm Emanuel and it has gotten him in trouble. In one of the issues that I actually agree with him on, he challenged the teachers' unions on their monopoly of education and their keeping charter schools out. When a charter comes to town, it is greeted by hostility and legal obstructions by the teachers unions, despite the proven effectiveness of moving students out of Chicago's slums. In charter schools far more not only graduate, but go on to college, they also contribute in lowering the crime rate altogether. Even the contender for Emanuel's slot hasn't made any commitments to support the teacher unions over charter schools, he said he would consider it. I guess to some people, not saying no means yes.

NAKED DISCLOSURE

Another baffling thing about progressives is their criteria for determining who is worthy of protection. A rape of a former adult movie star–in front of her children, in her home–is apparently not important to progressives because of her chosen profession. She works to titillate men, the feminist enemy, so she must pay the price. A human being was *physically violated and her occupation is all that matters!* What is wrong with these people?

It's not just the feminists that are this way either, race agitators go insane at the sight of a black conservative. They are the

Republican Party's "black friend" as Toure put it, or as so many have referred to them as "Uncle Tom's", traitors to the race as they see it.

The teacher's union has blood on their hands from this as well, with women like Cristy Nicole, Victoria Jackson or Katie Pearson. All three women worked in education and have also worked as models, and all three had their jobs put in jeopardy because of their modeling. They violated "code of decency" rules, that I'm sure they weren't even directly informed of. Victoria at the time, hadn't done any nude modeling when the school board suspended her. Now some of you readers might think I'm defending these women, well I guess I kind of am, the school board did overreact in my opinion. If they had done worse or were bad at their jobs, I would be more comfortable with their decisions. After their firings their students went to their defense on social media. It is the students that are the most harmed here, and that's where the teacher's union was in the wrong. The students defended them, their union did not. The teacher's union will defend the worst racists, radical extremists and pedophiles' jobs, but these and other women who violated "codes of decency", and did no *legitimate* harm to anyone lose their jobs. From progressives we can only learn that a victim is only a victim if they say so.

SAVE THE CLEVELAND INDIANS

As with specific events, like the Trayvon Martin shooting, there are times that I think an issue won't blow up and end up very wrong. It never ceases to amaze me how deep the well of social victimhood can sink. The movement to censor athletic teams with "culturally insensitive" names is in the category of the insane in Victim Culture. That's why it wasn't exactly surprising, but more a surreal stupidity moment when I heard the progressives were trying to legally force sports teams like the Cleveland Indians and Washington Redskins to change their names. Here's the thing, before the progressive push on this, we didn't hear much on this issue, and afterwards, that's when people got offended. That's why I was hoping it would not have gotten as far as it did. To show my disgust with the issue, I posted a picture of myself wearing a Cleveland Indians ball cap with the hashtag #savetheclevelandindians headline in the picture.

PROGRESSIVES DON'T HATE WAR, BUT WANT TO CONTROL IT

I get a lot of emails from political groups asking me to sign this petition and that, for or against a variety of causes. There has been a distinct pattern in the format of the petitions depending on who they are from. The notices from anti-union groups, second amendment defenders, and from the super PAC's of Rand Paul, end with a clear letter stating their agenda in bulletin points. It's open and upfront what they want done and the message being sent. Progressive groups like CREDO or Demand Progress are far less so detailed. Some would dismiss this as harmless but it's not. One of these messages was to sign a petition that supposedly tied the president's hands when it came to the declaration of war powers. It was pushed by Barbara Lee a democrat representing California, this is a battle she has struggled with since the September 11 attack in 2001, when Bush pledged to find the attackers at any cost. Her understanding of the Constitution and war powers is correct, it's the congress that decides whether we go to war. The fact that she is being critical of Obama as well as Bush, would also be very inviting for independents, but don't RSVP just yet. She has a big time agenda here that is less about war and more to do with increasing her personal power. Lee wants to create a new Department, the Department of Peace and Nonviolence. Nonviolence and Peace, who could oppose that? That's a common progressive tactic, make things sound innocuous or even benevolent, but there is always more to it. In this case the fine print is in what else is in the bill. First it's establishment and functions:

TITLE I—ESTABLISHMENT OF

DEPARTMENT OF PEACE AND NONVIOLENCE

SEC. 101. ESTABLISHMENT OF DEPARTMENT OF PEACE AND NONVIOLENCE.

(a) ESTABLISHMENT
.—There is hereby established a Department of Peace and Nonviolence (hereinafter in this Act referred to as the ''Department''), which shall—

(1) be a cabinet-level department in the executive branch of the Federal Government; and

(2) be dedicated to peacemaking and the study of conditions that are conducive to both domestic and international peace.

(b) SECRETARY OF PEACE AND NONVIOLENCE
.— There shall be at the head of the Department a Secretary of Peace and Nonviolence (hereinafter in this Act referred to as the ''Secretary''), who shall be appointed by the President, with the advice and consent of the Senate.

(c) MISSION

—The Department shall—

(1) hold peace as an organizing principle, coordinating service to every level of American society;

(2) endeavor to promote justice and democratic principles to expand human rights;

(3) strengthen nonmilitary means of peace-making;

(4) promote the development of human potential;

(5) work to create peace, prevent violence, divert from armed conflict, use field-tested programs, and develop new structures in nonviolent dispute resolution;

(6) take a proactive, strategic approach in the development of policies that promote national and international conflict prevention, nonviolent intervention, mediation, peaceful resolution of conflict, and structured mediation of conflict;

(7) address matters both domestic and inter-national in scope; and

(8) encourage the development of initiatives from local communities, religious groups, and nongovernmental organizations.

SEC. 102. RESPONSIBILITIES AND POWERS.

(a) IN GENERAL
.—The Secretary shall—

(1) work proactively and interactively with each branch of the Federal Government on all policy matters relating to conditions of peace;

(2) serve as a delegate to the National Security Council;

(3) call on the intellectual and spiritual wealth of the people of the United States and seek participation in its administration and in its development of policy from private, public, and nongovernmental organizations; and

(4) monitor and analyze causative principles of
conflict and make policy recommendations for developing and maintaining peaceful conduct.

(b) DOMESTIC RESPONSIBILITIES .—The Secretary shall—

(1) develop policies that address domestic violence, including spousal abuse, child abuse, and mistreatment of the elderly;

(2) create new policies and incorporate existing programs that reduce drug and alcohol abuse;

(3) develop new policies and incorporate existing policies regarding crime, punishment, and rehabilitation;

(4) develop policies to address violence against animals;

(5) analyze existing policies, employ successful, field-tested programs, and develop new approaches for dealing with the implements of violence, including gun-related violence and the overwhelming presence of handguns;

(6) develop new programs that relate to the societal challenges of school violence, gangs, racial or ethnic violence, violence against gays and lesbians, and police-community relations disputes;

(7) make policy recommendations to the Attorney General regarding civil rights and labor law;

(8) assist in the establishment and funding of community-based violence prevention programs, including violence prevention counseling and peer mediation in schools;

(9) counsel and advocate on behalf of women victimized by violence;

(10) provide for public education programs and counseling strategies concerning hate crimes;

(11) promote racial, religious, and ethnic tolerance;

(12) finance local community initiatives that can draw on neighborhood resources to create peace
projects that facilitate the development of conflict resolution at a national level and thereby inform and inspire national policy; and

(13) provide ethical-based and value-based analyses to the Department of Defense.

INTERNATIONAL RESPONSIBILITIES .—The Secretary shall—

(1) advise the Secretary of Defense and the Secretary of State on all matters relating to national security, including the protection of human rights and the prevention of, amelioration of, and de-escalation of unarmed and armed international conflict;

(2) provide for the training of all United States
personnel who administer postconflict reconstruction and demobilization in war-torn societies;

(3) sponsor country and regional conflict prevention and dispute resolution initiatives, create special task forces, and draw on local, regional, and national expertise to develop plans and programs for addressing the root sources of conflict in troubled areas;

(4) provide for exchanges between the United States and other nations of individuals who endeavor to develop domestic and international peace-based initiatives;

(5) encourage the development of international sister city programs, pairing

United States cities with cities around the globe for artistic, cultural, economic, educational, and faith-based exchanges;

(6) administer the training of civilian peace-keepers who participate in multinational nonviolent police forces and support civilian police who participate in peacekeeping;

(7) jointly with the Secretary of theTreasury, strengthen peace enforcement through hiring and training monitors and investigators to help with the enforcement of international arms embargoes;

(8) facilitate the development of peace summits at which parties to a conflict may gather under carefully prepared conditions to promote nonviolent communication and mutually beneficial solutions;

(9) submit to the President recommendations for reductions in weapons of mass destruction, and make annual reports to the President on the sale of arms from the United States to other nations, with analysis of the impact of such sales on the defense of the United States and how such sales

affect peace;

(10) in consultation with the Secretary of State, develop strategies for sustainability and management of the distribution of international funds; and

(11) advise the United States Ambassador to the United Nations on matters pertaining to the United Nations Security Council.

(d) HUMAN SECURITY RESPONSIBILITIES

.

—The Secretary shall address and offer nonviolent conflict resolution strategies to all relevant parties on issues of human security if such security is threatened by conflict, whether such conflict is geographic, religious, ethnic, racial, or class-based in its origin, derives from economic concerns (including trade or maldistribution of wealth), or is initiated through disputes concerning scarcity of natural resources (such as water and energy resources),food, trade, or environmental concerns.

(e) MEDIA RELATED
RESPONSIBILITIES
.

—Respecting the first amendment of the
Constitution of the United States and the
requirement for free and independent media,
the Secretary shall—

(1) seek assistance in the design and
implementation of nonviolent policies from
media professionals;

(2) study the role of the media in the
escalation and de-escalation of conflict at
domestic and international levels and make
findings public; and

(3) make recommendations to professional
media organizations in order to provide
opportunities to increase media awareness of
peace-building initiatives.

(f) EDUCATIONAL RESPONSIBILITIES

.—The Secretary shall—

(1) develop a peace education curriculum,
which

shall include studies of—

(A) the civil rights movement in the United States and throughout the world, with special emphasis on how individual endeavor and involvement have contributed to advancements in peace and justice; and

(B) peace agreements and circumstances in which peaceful intervention has worked to stop conflict;

(2) in cooperation with the Secretary of Education—

(A) commission the development of such curricula and make such curricula available to local school districts to enable the utilization of peace education objectives at all elementary and secondary schools in the United States; and

(B) offer incentives in the form of grants and training to encourage the development of State peace curricula and assist schools in applying for such curricula;

(3) work with educators to equip students to

become skilled in achieving peace through reflection, and facilitate instruction in the ways of peaceful conflict resolution;

(4) maintain a site on the Internet for the purposes of soliciting and receiving ideas for the development of peace from the wealth of political, social and cultural diversity;

(5) proactively engage the critical thinking capabilities of grade school, high school, and college students and teachers through the Internet and other media and issue periodic reports concerning submissions;

(6) create and establish a Peace Academy, which shall—

(A) be modeled after the military service academies;

(B) provide a 4-year course of instruction in peace education, after which graduates will be required to serve 5 years in public service in programs dedicated to domestic or international nonviolent conflict resolution; and

(7) provide grants for peace studies departments in colleges and universities throughout the United States.

SEC. 103. PRINCIPAL OFFICERS.

(a) UNDER SECRETARY OF PEACE AND NONVIOLENCE

.—There shall be in the Department an Under Secretary of Peace and Nonviolence, who shall be appointed by the President, by and with the advice and consent of the Senate. During the absence or disability of the Secretary, or in the event of a vacancy in the office of the Secretary, the Under Secretary shall act as Secretary.
The Secretary shall designate the order in which other officials of the Department shall act for and perform the functions of the Secretary during the absence or disability of both the Secretary and Under Secretary or in the event of vacancies in both of those offices.

So, who will enforce all this?

(b) ADDITIONAL POSITIONS
.
—(1) There shall be in the Department—

(A) an Assistant Secretary for Peace Education and Training;

(B) an Assistant Secretary for Domestic Peace Activities;

(C) an Assistant Secretary for International Peace Activities;

(D) an Assistant Secretary for Technology for Peace;

(E) an Assistant Secretary for Arms Control and Disarmament;

 (F) an Assistant Secretary for Peaceful Coexistence and Nonviolent Conflict Resolution;

(G) an Assistant Secretary for Human and Economic Rights; and

(H) a General Counsel.

Getting more control of education, the internet, further intervention in the economy, more spending, extending gun control, more victims, I think this bill covers it all. Plus Lee gets a free pass, since she criticized both Bush and Obama. To all those who would consider this bill because of that, read the fine print, like most laws it's got an unsavory after taste.

JUST SAYIN'

So this is the world based on progressive thought, that we are all victims and owe the different demographics for the actions of the long dead, or to acquiesce to the United Nation, or complete control of the internet. It doesn't end there.

There is a campaign with the agenda to replace Andrew Jackson on the twenty dollar bill and replace him with a feminist activist, to be officially decided on later. The candidates include–Susan B. Anthony; Rosa Parks; anti-slavery activist Sojourner Truth; Harriet Tubman; the first woman of the U.S. Cabinet, Frances Perkins; Congresswomen:

Patsy Mink, Shirley Chrisholm, and Barbara Jordan; Eleanor Roosevelt; Margaret Sanger, a birth control activist; environmental activist, Rachel Carson; feminist Betty Friedan; and Clara Barton, founder of the Red Cross.

The Women on $20s non-profit, has had big support by actress Susan Sarandon, and even Barack Obama is on board, saying it sounds like it's "a pretty good idea." The group's executive director, Susan Ades Stone, was "sort of surprised at the lack of opposition" to the effort–receiving 8,000 votes within the first 60 hours. "We want to be the hashtag that says #sorryAndrew," Stone continues.

The obvious reason for this is reparation for women–and notably, black women–for the years of not being properly represented. The problem with this claim, it's not exactly true; Susan B. Anthony was on a coin until 1981, Helen Keller and Sacagawea are currently on coinage today. The real contention here isn't having a woman on a coin or paper dollar; it's the clear message sent of having women with contributions to society that are so controversial. Helen Keller, while making enormous strides for those with physical impairments, was a devout socialist and Eleanor Roosevelt was an extremist in all aspects of social justice. It's not an issue of having a woman on the dollar but does their contribution proportionately out-weigh those of the President they are calling to remove? Hardly, even with Old Hickory's human rights violations in the Trail of Tears; his dismantling of the Second National Bank and balancing the budget puts his actions "with good results" in the lead against these women's "good intentions."

Another odd thing about all this; their target, the founder of the Democratic Party Andrew Jackson. Why would they possibly be trying to erase him from history, in the same manner a new Pharaoh would the legacy of the previous ruler? It could be as simple as damage control for the baggage associated with Jackson. Jackson shows plainly the inherent hypocrisy in the party, but for that conclusion to really make sense will they do the same to Woodrow Wilson or Lyndon Johnson? At this time the real goal for going after Jackson will remain a mystery; much as the logic behind most of the decisions made by the social democrats. With all the enabling by progressives, encouraging new non-victims and inventing ever more creative forms of social contention–I hope it's a little more clear why enemas for all of them is the best solution. Just sayin'!

CHAPTER TEN

SELECTIVE VICTIMS

It's a strong showing that the

Progressives really don't care about their causes, but marketing them. If they did, these cases wouldn't have fallen through the cracks.

PROTECTING THE FREAKS FROM EXPLOITATION

Even if you aren't an activist looking to fix all the "wrongs" of society, you probably agree with the Victims Culture crowd when it comes to the Freak Shows. Freak Shows or Side shows have been–still are even now–a part of popular culture and for many, something the populous wish never had been. People on display, like animals, with animal names for a lot of them. Medical oddities and attractions like the Fiji Mermaid–which was later proven a hoax–and exotic beasts from around the world. All in chains or otherwise secured, how can this *not* be considered slavery? Whoa now!–Settle down and put down that glass of emotional reactionaryism, I think you've had enough. This is one more time when you're letting emotion overrule logic.

While I didn't necessarily argue about people's sentiments about the issue, my curiosity was always stronger; and I wanted to find out more about people like Robert Ripley and P.T. Barnum, and their traveling oddities. I learned something very important about Victim culture when it came to the side shows–and in general really–that for the most part, it's a greater piece of fiction than the Fiji Mermaid! Those who condemn Barnum as an exploiter of the humans in his shows didn't understand the truly amazing and humane thing he did for these people–he employed them. How many other people would have done that? More importantly, how could they do the jobs anyway? When you're talking someone without legs, there was extremely limited opportunities during the reign of the side show. Even fully capable freaks like Cheng and Eng, the Siamese Twins, would have had a hard go at getting work anywhere else. Besides, the claim of exploitation is not even close to being true anyway, they weren't in chains and free to move about and were fully compensated for their performances. Not only were they given a salary, but room and board—which kept them *separate* from the cruel world. *That was an act of humanity not exploitation!* The freak shows were a way to bring the world to those who never could have seen it otherwise; but it was so much more for those with deformities—it was a job and it was a home.

GUN CONTROL HURTS THE DISABLED
When the Aurora shooting occurred,

the call for gun control rang out loud and clear–again, but this time it was a little different, this time it was focused, it had a particle demographic in mind–the mentally disabled. The "logic" employed here was that "the mentally handicapped had to be protected from themselves and society," the odd thing is, it appears there's very few who have disagreed! Yes there are those who are dangerous to society when a firearm is in their hands, but that has *nothing* to do with mental retardation.

The Aurora shooter was mentally unstable *not* handicapped, so why push the issue with the claim he was? It was all part of the plan to reinforce a measure in the Affordable Care Act, that a doctor can declare someone mentally unstable and have their guns taken from them. Used in conjunction with another part of the law where your doctor is required to ask if you possess any firearms, the government can keep tabs on the nation's gun owners and if deemed a threat, have them labeled a threat because of diminished capacity. So the question for you is, are you now mentally disabled?

S.W.A.T.TED

One point of agreement that I have with progressives, is that police can be extreme in their actions and that the law encourages bad behavior. Where we differ is who is to blame: they blame the cops, I blame the government. This is important to get cleared up, because the solution is different depending on who's at fault. If it's the police, we need more federal oversight; if the government, we need reforms in the laws. Where progressives lose their logical advantage is that pretty much every case of misconduct has a legal statute that the officers involved were following. That shows that something is wrong in our legal system itself. No-knock warrants, are an example of this; take the case of Chad Chadwicke, the man who was violated by the legal system, not only by this bad law, but also when he was trying to get justice for the mistake.

Civil Asset Forfeiture is another example of a bad law with egregious consequences. An officer can confiscate your belongings while during an investigation and is under no legal obligation to return them, even if you're found not guilty or the officer is at fault.

NO JUSTICE ONLY PIECES

The Trayvon Martin incident was still comparatively fresh when Michael Brown was shot by police officer Darren Wilson. With the palatable anger in Ferguson, Missouri—further enflamed by the likes of Al Sharpton and Jesse Jackson—it was only a matter of time before violence occurred. Violence against people and property; the mindless mob turned to looting the city. What exactly this has to do with "getting justice" for these shootings is obvious only to the perpetrators.

Natalie Dubose was a businesswoman in

Ferguson during the worst of the attacks on the city and her business suffered great physical damage at the hands of these passionate marauders. She did nothing wrong and is a black woman, but that didn't save her from their wrath. In trying to find "justice" for the "victims", Martin and Brown, they were complacently blind to the fact they made far more *genuine* victims. As for Dubose, her story doesn't have an entirely bad ending; she started a campaign on social media asking for donations to rebuild with the results being she got far more from generous donors than her goal. Charity and capitalism, once again, proves to be the better solution than government largesse.

7 MONTHS TOO LONG

When terrorists recently murdered one of its citizens of the country of Jordan their president took immediate action. He had the two terrorists linked to the fire–that took the Jordanian's life–and they were executed. This was a very strong demonstration of strength by their leader that has always been absent in the Obama playbook; take the country of Mexico holding Marine Sargent Tahmooressi hostage. While the two incidents are not the same, and are not deserving the same level of force– at least the Jordanian president showed true leadership.

In the last two administrations we have seen the two extremes–when it comes to force–against other countries demonstrating hostility towards the US, and our reaction to it. President Bush took the over-kill approach, vow a vendetta against the attackers and damn the conduct in its pursuit. It made the country look like a bully in the end and we alienated nations that would have made the search for the culprits easier. Our current leader took to the other extreme, *ignore the very existence* of the threat to our nation and blame the US for it. This argument basically gives their ideology more credibility than it deserves. I disagree with our attempts to "fix" these nations; but this dangerous assertion is more of a blatant blame of the victim. They attack us and we turn around and apologize for it. The better way to make our nation safe is *not to invade their country*, but to place those troops around *our borders*. The Reagan approach in negotiations with Russia gave a model to work with in this kind of situation. Only attack those who are valid, call out those who deserve it and let everyone–friend and foe alike–know that what you say you will do. Don't say that you will "draw a line in the sand' if you have no intention of backing that up, but don't act in a manner that will disengage those who could be of assistance in the agenda.

THE UNWELCOME SIGN

Many times the calls of racism is another thing altogether. Take immigration–when immigration is brought up its called racist, it's not but it could be considered xenophobic. Our national consensus on immigrants hasn't always been positive. The earliest showing of legal policy of such animosity was under John Adams and the *Alien and Sedition Acts*. It's actually rather difficult to understand these acts–what exactly is the connection between immigration and freedom of speech?–but the consequences, were severe for both.

When the railroads started crossing the country the nation needed a large crop of workers; President Lincoln imported Chinese laborers for the project. That did not sit well with American workers and the earliest unions formed. Ever since then whenever there has been a dispute in labor that involves immigrants, it has been spearheaded by unions–until now.

Now the unions have started protecting the immigrants rather than their union members. Most of the accusations of racism in the immigration realm are made by Mexicans but whenever either legal status is questioned, that's an easy distraction. But this anger has been directed at *any* immigrant, in many cases towards whites. When the Irish immigrants came to this country at the start of the industrial revolution, they were treated just as badly as any of the minorities. Anyone who enters the country should be treated with a welcome sign if they went through the system, whether they are *union* or not.

DILLION TAYLOR GETS LOST

How many of you reading this are familiar with the name, Michael Brown? How about Trayvon Martin? Or Eric Garner? Okay, now have you ever heard of Dillion Taylor? No? Of course you haven't because unlike the others mentioned, he wasn't in the national dialogue and for one reason–he was a *white* guy, killed by a *black* cop. This is the scenario in which you really get "no justice, no peace" because you're not even worth the time. With the others mentioned here the officers were questioned about the conduct or laws involved with their cases, that's a good thing but they were overshadowed by the identity politics championed by the likes of Al Sharpton and Jesse Jackson. Taylor wasn't even given that much. To be fair his case was mentioned in the headlines, but just as quickly dismissed. The *Huffington Post* has numerous articles on the others, only one on Taylor. In a lot of the *major* news he's not mentioned at all.

Whenever there is a questionable death of someone, there should be an inquiry, there should be anger and the important questions asked. That's the problem, though, the important questions aren't asked, in most of the mentioned cases all there is, is the anger. In his own part of the country Taylor's friends and family stand alone, trying to get justice for the man whose case has just as many questions about the conduct of the officer involved as Brown and Garner, but since he was born white those questions might never get asked. I'm not saying that people should going around protesting like they did in Ferguson, frankly, what they did there was indefensible. I'm also not saying that the officers involved were in the wrong, I don't know for sure and that's the point. From what I have read there were valid concerns of possible misconduct and that *should* have been the context of the discussion not the context of identity politics, but was the amount of force used appropriate? If you make it about as divisive and inclusive an issue as racism, then you end up losing a major part of the population in your support to find out the truth–if that is what you really care about.

WHAT NOT HAVING AN OPINION CAN GET YOU

David Autry was just minding his own business on his way home, when he had a violent encounter with three black youth on a St. Louis train car. What was the cause of the attack? Had he made some racial slur at one of them? Had he tried to "stare them down?" Had he scuffed one of their "kicks?" None of the above–he simply wanted to be left alone and three teens wanted to discuss

Michael Brown. He said he had no opinion on the matter and was hoping that was it, but what followed was a very brutal and unprovoked assaulted on Gentry. The video was posted on YouTube "and got tons of reactions to it," Gentry recalls. "The first, of course, is horror that this level of violence is now the norm in places like St. Louis." He recounts the attack saying, "I was dazed from the sucker punch in the face... C'mon three against one? I was trying to protect my glasses. I didn't know they were on the floor... If I had ... fought [back, being] the only white guy on that train car, how do I know I wouldn't have been attacked from behind."

Jesse Lee Peterson, a black activist and civil rights leader and founder of the Brotherhood Organization of a New Destiny isn't at all surprised by this and blames the Obama administration for it. "This ... black on white attack in St. Louis [is] another example of the growing racially motivated violence against white folks... Barack

Obama, Eric Holder and the other so-called civil rights leaders have given blacks the justification to attack whites." A sentiment that is made clear by Malik Shebazz, the leader of the New Black Panthers, the "justice department leadership is in the hands of a black man by the name of Eric Holder," when asked about the failure to indict the Black Panthers of charges of voter intimidation. I don't agree with BOND on all its stances, but on this one we do see eye to eye.

A KILLER UNIVERSITY

With the nation outraged by the calls for "No Justice, No Peace" another person was pushed aside by the sleeping media. A college sophomore at Virginia University, Hannah Graham was murdered by a black man, named Jesse L. Matthews Jr. Her body was found in the woods outside of Albemarle County, VA in October, 2014. It was surmised by authorities that Matthews was the last to see the young woman alive;

the attack said to have occurred in September of that year. When Matthews was announced as a person of interest, he fled to Texas where he was apprehended.

But Graham wasn't Matthews' only victim, he was linked forensically to another woman's death in Fairfax. Virginia Tech student Morgan Harrington disappeared after leaving a Metallica concert performed at Virginia U in 2009. At this time he hasn't been charged with Harrington's death.

MORE VICTIMS OF NON-WHITE MALES

Anthony Roberts, aged 26, of Middlebury left a Lansdowne man dead and his wife in critical condition after their 2009 attack. Included in the list of charges: robbery, aggravated malicious wounding and rape. Roberts wasn't alone that night, when he attacked the couple during their nightly walk. Jamie Ayala, 23, and David Bowman, 22, have been charged, but Roberts was suspected as the instigator of the assault. The victims, retired Army couple, William and Cynthia Bennett were found in a Lansdowne road separated by 50 miles. The trauma surgeon testified that that with Cynthia's injuries, it was a medical miracle she survived.

Then there was the Jena Six, a case of six black teens beating a white kid in Jena, Louisiana. The race agitators claimed that the Jena Six were the real victims because they were the lower numbers in the school at only 10% black to 90% white. What a cop-out! So what if they were the smaller percentage of the populace, that doesn't give them the right to assault another human being without consequences. Another part of the sob story was there were other incidents that led up to it; a rope hung from a swing, confrontations between blacks and whites, and a fire in the main building. Those were not targeted toward the Jena Six though, in fact the rope noose was a message to the *white sports teams*. Another criticism was they were treated differently by police because they were black, that could be true and if so, that is wrong. Was it the case though? They might have been singled out not because of the color of their skin, but the severity and volume of their crimes. Whatever the case may be, it lead to the "largest civil rights demonstration in years" according to the BBC, with between 15,000-20,000 protesters.

A RELIGION OF PEACE?

Kayla Mueller, 26, was killed after being held hostage by the Islamic State in Syria. ISIL (the Islamic State) claimed she had been killed when a Jordanian jet bombed the group's de facto capital Raqqa. This claim has been met with scrutiny by the US and Jordan officials, with Jordanians stating that the target, in question, served as a "weapons compound" which would make holding a hostage there highly dubious.

"The information that we have … is that there was no evidence of civilians in the target area," Josh Earnest, White House press secretary replies. A Prescott, Arizona native, Mueller was in the Syrian city of Aleppo helping refugees escape the country's civil war, when in August 2013, she was abducted.

CHAPTER ELEVEN

ICONOMY

Part of the causes of the problems

in our Victim Culture comes from the entitlements systems. The entitlements system is the tool used to advance their social control.

PLANNED PROFITHOOD

Abortion is a horrible thing that should be limited but putting it in the hands of the federal government, is not the way to do that. In fact they seem to increase the numbers. Why? That's complicated, and it has more than one answer. Part of it has to do with population control (something I covered in *UNConventional Wisdom*) and part of it has to do with government pandering, if they get to do both at the same time, the more the better. In the world of politics the incentives are not to work together, but to pit the two major parties against each other and get out of the way. Think of it as a giant cock fight, the two birds claw and peck at each other in the ring until one is defeated, at least that's how it works sometimes, most of the time the republicans just cave in on the issues and let the democrats do their thing.

That was how we ended up with Obamacare and why–like a rotten smell–we can't get rid of it! The republicans would rather "play nice" than risk being labeled as mean. I don't think you were elected to be nice with the party of the jackass, but to tell them no. Under Obamacare 115,000 federally funded abortions will be performed and Planned Parenthood–a non-profit, that is supposed to be helping women make the best reproductive decisions, not advocating abortion as the only choice–will be making a lot of money from the deal and you helped it happen. Thank you, I'm sure they will be so happy. Actually, I'm sure they will say that they want more, because government cronyism only encourages want and not restraint.

SANDRA FLUKED

If you want to see a clear example that the Democratic Party has *completely* lost their way, look no further than Sandra Fluke. This attorney had the headlines by saying the Affordable Care Act should cover birth control. This is actually a little absurd, having an *attorney*–and a well-connected one at that–to come out and ask for her contraceptives to be covered by insurance. She has money–pay for them herself!

"[Fluke] essentially says that she must be paid to have sex–what does that make her? It makes her a slut, right? It makes her a prostitute. She wants to be paid to have sex.

She's having so much sex she can't afford the contraception. She wants you and me and the taxpayers to pay her to have sex." Those were the comments made by Rush Limbaugh that he later did a forced apology for. Yes, I'm being inflammatory and yes, she's not talking about freebies for her. Well, not just for her, she's calling for free birth control for all womankind, because with all the oppression from us men–they deserve it. For the record, the birth control in question, is *not* free–as Limbaugh reminded us–but taxpayer funded. This is of little importance to Obama or Fluke, they get to further increase the democratic base and add more laws, and Fluke gets more political clout. Limbaugh is right about Fluke, she truly is an Obama whore, she used her prestige to campaign for him and his policies including the Lily Ledbetter Fair Pay Act and the Affordable Care Act. This anonymous attorney has shown how far she is willing to sleep her way to the top, by running for political office in California.

Will it end there? Hope so, the Fluke presidency sounds like a national disaster– thankfully she won't have any children to pass her ideology to.

Fluke is doing all this to get attention, maybe she wasn't getting enough attention so she went on the air and said she was "giving it away for free" or maybe she did do it entirely to sleep her way to the top. If it's the latter, she should be trying to get that written off as tax deduction–not a health care concern–since her whoring herself has seemed to have become a "business as usual" style of career advancement with her.

IT'S A SNAP

Probably the most abused entitlement program is the food stamps program, SNAP. Remember the slacker rock star that dines on lobster, while you're eating mac and cheese? Who paid for it? The taxpayer, you and I, doesn't that make you a little angry? It does me! How is it fair, that those that acted with fiscal discipline have to supplement those who don't even understand the basics of economics? What makes this all worse is that they actually believe they deserve it– since they are contemporary bohemians and contribute arts to the national community. That was the entire selling point of the program, after all. It was set up so the artists, can "focus on their arts." In the art world, principles are completely pragmatic, if your ethics interferes with your "masterpiece" by all means ignore them.

That's a philosophy that has worked wonders in the past, ask Dr., Peter Singer, a big advocate of "Practical Ethics" or H.G. Wells who would have gladly had the "inferiors" amongst us exterminated. When people offer the challenge to demonstrate the socialization of America, the Iconomy is it. The Iconomy doesn't foster creativity but instead parasitic, rampant sloth. It's a system of systematic laziness and stupidity where the government enslaves you into a welfare zombie and discourages you from ever leaving. Once you are in the welfare state, you're here forever!

HOUSEWIVES NEED A UNION

Should wives be given compensation for the work they do? For the most part they do–if the marriage is a solid, stable one. In successful marriages, decisions are made together and the source of such a contentious attitude comes from the feminist sects of America who think of marriage as enslavement. Why would anyone listen to someone who has the agenda to destroy a happy home? That's like asking a robber to housesit. Oh, and please don't take our computer and TV, we kind of need them to get stupid advice from stupid people who don't really know anything.

UGLY PEOPLE AND SMELLY CABBIES

With so many already under the victimhood umbrella, it has become necessary for the enablers to find new avenues of the non-oppressed oppressed, enter the uglies and smelly. The glimpse into the future has shown this will be the where they go next, the unattractive in sight and smell will now be heard. The future will be an ugly place indeed.

PLAYING HARP

With the abysmal failure of Fanny Mae and Freddy Mac and the entire housing market bubble still comparatively fresh in people's minds, you would imagine that lawmakers–if not the general public– would be hesitant to try this scheme again, but here we go again! HARP is open for business and so are the sketchy restrictions and non-existent laws to protect the country from a repeat performance of the housing bubble. In the Iconomy this is way things are done though, there's no learning from your mistakes, *the only mistake was going too small!* This time, go bigger and the mistakes of the past will be avoided. Even thinking about this is giving me a headache!

Look people, if something sounds too good, then it usually is–if you can't afford to buy a house, then don't buy a house. I know that to some this sounds downright un-American, but not everyone is meant to be homeowners. There is nothing wrong with staying in apartments or townhomes, it doesn't make you a failure, as some people might think. Its better you don't buy a house or wait and save up than get hurt by this reoccurring scheme. *But wait a minute, doesn't the lender take all the risk? HARP loans are not government loans after all and the lending institution will be held entirely responsible in the case of default?* That's what they said last time too and a lot of people had to foreclose. HARP loans are services provided by private institutions, yes, but only *in part*. The government is still partially involved, which means don't go in blindly or you could end up falling off a financial cliff.

GOING TO BANKS

Accompanying her nude pictorial spread in *Playboy* magazine's April release, rapper Azealia Banks also made very contentious statements about the United States. "I hate everything about this country. I hate fat white Americans," she goes on. "All the people who are crunched into … America are these racist conservative white people who live on their farms. Those little teenage girls who work at Kmart and have a racist grandma – that's really America."

Where does the 23-year-old Harlem native get her animosity for the country? From "the streets"–where else? "The black kids got in trouble all the time. We were loud or whatever, but whenever she told a white kid to quiet down and they did, she'd be like, whatever. But if she told a black kid to quiet down and one of them sucked their teeth, she'd put them in the corner." Somewhere along the way Banks got it in her head that the whole world would bow down before her feet and she practiced on "a teacher I could not stand" she says. Her second grade class kept journals and she "wrote in the journal one day, 'I can't stand this white bitch teacher…. She found my journal and called my mother, who was embarrassed, because my mother used to say stuff like that–'White people are the devil. Stay away from them.' That teacher was scared of me after that." Maybe, or maybe she was ashamed of her. Who really knows, but this is not the first time the "Ice Princess" has shown her instructors that "she's the boss." In the interview she brags about punching a teacher in the face when she was 3 while attending preschool. "People have always been scared of me. We were playing house, and the lady was like 'I'm a monster! I'm gonna eat your family' I punched her right in the eye."

She goes on about "the generational effects of Jim Crowe and poverty [that] linger on" and her goal of getting … out of here and … leave y'all to your own devices." But first she wants money, lots of it and rather than be generous to her fans and enjoy her fame she taunts them and says she is owed reparations. "My little white fans will be like, 'Why do you want reparations for work you didn't do?' Well, you got handed down your grandfather's estate and … your grandmother's diamonds and pearls." Yes, the picked on rapper who is the one who *could really* afford the "diamonds and pearls" touting the same old, boring line of the world owes me because I'm black. I'm repressed because it's easier to claim that than actually doing something worthwhile. Like many blacks who feel "owed" she also doesn't want to have a real discussion about race. Yeah, I am loud and boisterous [,] … black, and … a pain in your ass. But I'm not really talking to you, and that's what makes those people mad. You're not invited to this conversation…When you rip people from their land [,]… customs [,] … culture– there's … a piece of me that knows I'm not supposed to be speaking English, I'm not supposed to be worshipping Jesus Christ. All this … is unnatural to me."

Her hostility towards black "sell-outs" has

been extremely vocal as well, saying the goal "is to be a nonthreatening black person" and that artists like Pharrell and Kendrick Lamar when they say things like– "How can we expect people to respect us if we don't respect ourselves?" Banks assesses them as "playing that nonthreatening black man ... that gets all the white soccer moms going 'We love him.' ... 'Please accept me, white world.'" Banks continues, "In my adulthood I'm having to destroy all these things society really wants you to think. The history textbooks in the U.S. are the worse if you're not white. Young black kids should have their own special curriculum... All you know as a black kid is we came here on a boat, we didn't have anything, and we still don't have anything." Banks is a physical representation of everything that is the perpetual victim, one obsessed with anger at those who did nothing wrong to her and she doesn't care to become more knowledgeable but is more content being a malcontent.

FINDING YOURSELF

Finding yourself, I can't think of anything more selfish than the goal of finding yourself. Not because it's not easy to get lost or that finding your purpose is always apparent right out of high school, but because of the commonly accepted game-plan involved. You're just out of high school, up until this point school has really been all you know–some might have had summer jobs or had work release–and now you're thrust into the world, so what's next? Do you go right to school? Get a job? Or take a year off and get your plan formalized? For far too many, it's none of the above and that's because they have to "find themselves."

I get and applaud the taking some time to figure things out, I wish I had, but I rushed into school and ended up bailing out, but that's not what a lot of people are doing. They are taking extended vacations from life, no school, no work, or *even considering* either, just wasting their lives being worthless losers. Even when I wasn't in school I at least had a job or was looking for one! That's called being an adult and responsible, yeah, it sucks sometimes, but shut up and do it! It's because of those who are "finding themselves" that taxes are higher than they should be, because while they are "lost" they are taking advantage of subsidies; or they are costing society because they aren't helping expand another dream, or better yet, creating their own. Finding yourself–next time you cry about needing to "find yourself" why don't you get lost.

CHAPTER TWELVE

DREAMS FROM MY FOUNDING FATHERS

When our nation's **founders came**

to this country they came up with one of
the most unique and amazing systems of
government–one of self-government. It
doesn't always solve every problem but it
does a far better job than any federal agency
does. Along the way the great men and
women made their mistakes, to some this
diminishes the good, to me it means they
were human. This chapter is about the
mistakes they made–some may have simply
been rumors–and the impact those errors
had.

PRESIDENT JEFFERSON'S SECRET MISTRESS

As an ever increasing renewed interest in history has become more prevalent, there have been a lot of progressives who have taken it as an opportunity to advance their causes. It's through a very well thought through and brilliant plan of misrepresentation of history, rather than reporting it. Make the anti-federalists look like a group of secret society members or rich white men, who cared only about advancing their wealth. While it is true, that many of the founders had considerable fortunes, not all of them did. Thomas Jefferson was one of them. He also wasn't only in it for the money when it came to his slaves. He was a kind man towards them and treated them as family. One more than others, it is said.

Sometime after the death of his beloved wife, it's said that he started an affair with one of his slaves–with the end result being a lovechild. Did he have an affair with one of his slaves, an act that could put his fortune and livelihood in jeopardy? Yes, it's possible, but the more important question is; does it matter? I don't think so. With all the dirt that could be said about the founders, how can this be a threat to Jefferson's reputation? If anything it shows him as an even more complex human being. With the strict decorum of society in the colonial era it's hard to find a moment of vulnerable humanity from these great men. To me, this is nothing bad at all. He found solace and comfort with someone he was very familiar with and it shows his attitude towards the slaves were very complicated indeed.

THE EMANCIPATION NON-PARTICIPATION

We have the perspective that after the Civil War and with the Emancipation Proclamation signed, all of us, black, white, Mexican, Indian, or whatever race, we could get together and live in peace. Well... That wasn't *exactly* the plan, no. The Indians, were always meant to be by themselves on the reservations, the Mexicans back in Mexico, and the blacks were supposed to be shipped back to Africa. That was the original plan anyways; at least it was the plan of the Colonial founders, which included Jefferson (what I meant by the "his attitude towards the slaves were very complicated, indeed" remark at the end of the prior segment).

So what was Lincoln's solution to all this? He supported ending slavery but not integration. He believed that separation of the races was still the best idea, with all the fighting that occurs in our nation over race in Victim Culture, maybe he had a point!

ANDREW JOHNSON SCREWS US ALL

One of the worst pre-progressive era presidents would have to be Andrew Johnson; take all the racial superiority sentiments of all the founders, Andrew Jackson and Lincoln and you have Andrew Johnson summed up. But that's only a part

of the odiousness of Johnson's presidency–
the Lincoln assassination caused the other
part of it. If Lincoln had not been killed the
nation would have been better and in the end
it was the Confederate south that suffered
the most.

After the participants of the assassination
of Lincoln were executed, the south had to
pay the price for their years of slavery.
Johnson, a southern democrat and slavery
supporter, he would surely help them out,
right? Nope, in fact, Johnson didn't seem to
want to help ease anyone's burdens. The
Freedman's Bureau, a federal agency
established to help the freed slaves from
tormentors, was woefully underutilized and
the laws to protect the slaves were ignored
by the courts anyway. That didn't help the
South recover from the economic depression
that accompanied the end of slavery. This
depression and disenchantment, is what
caused a bunch of former Civil War soldiers
to form the Ku Klux Klan. It appears that
when it comes to unintended consequences

caused by apathy, Johnson's in a league of his own.

ANOTHER IMPORTANT WASHINGTON

With creeps like Jesse Jackson, Al Sharpton and Azealia Banks spouting idiotic declarations of reparations, it's always good to hear logical conclusions when it comes to race. Booker T. Washington was one of those men, his family was one of the last generations to have lived in slavery–which means he *actually* had good reason to think he was owed–but unlike the freed slaves of his time or their later relatives of the current generation, he didn't call for reparations. In fact he did the exact opposite; he saw that any outright activism would be greeted with violence. He went against the grain and led the example that in order to achieve freedom they had to earn it. Rather than trying to "get back what he was owed" he went out to make a name for himself; petitioning the greats of the industrial revolution for money to build the Tuskegee Institute–a school to advance those freed from slavery to be educated and teaching them to be self-reliant. On both sides Washington's way had its detractors, not only with groups like the Klan, but with the newly charted NAACP. We have examples, although only a few– unfortunately–of how race relations should be conducted. We would all be better off if we looked to Booker T. Washington, or Martin Luther King Jr. than Jackson or Sharpton.

A FRACTION OF A PERSON

Booker T. Washington was an anomaly when it came to the manner of former slaves having to earn their own way, but he wasn't alone. The famous orator, Frederick Douglass, thought that, but this wasn't as an apparent thought to Douglass. Douglass was actually a very amazing man, he taught himself to read and write, and passed that knowledge on to other slaves; he traveled to parts of Ireland and England, giving lectures; and he was able to raise enough funds to buy his freedom and start an abolitionist newspaper. It was when he was writing for this newspaper and with other abolitionist discussions that he started having an expansion of his thought process. Many of the other abolitionists were convinced that the U.S. Constitution was a racist document. At first, so too did Douglass, but a piece written by Lysander Spooner had caused Douglass to reevaluate his preconceived notions. This change of perspective caused a rift between Douglass and William Lloyd Garrison, an old friend, who had helped him. Garrison was one of the people that also convinced Douglass of the inherent racism within the Constitution and publicly burned copies of it.

Douglass was a known supporter of women's suffrage as well, making it clear that as a black man able to vote, it was wrong that a woman could not. Unlike most feminists, he took to the high road tactic of "be patient" and picked a more subtle and smart campaign of changing public opinion, rather than pushing for legal action. Douglass spent his life trying to change opinions on slavery and women's rights, not alienating others with contentious and contemptuous vitriol and gave us a better model–based on principle and knowledge–to work from.

WAS BIRTH OF THE NATION REALLY RACIST?

In the 1913, a silent film was released that would have a resonating long time influence within the White Power movement, and that was the film *Birth of a Nation.* At the time this movie was hailed as a triumphant marvel, a successful showing of a historically accurate portrait of history. It was even given high marks by President Woodrow Wilson. It has become known as the most racist film ever made and that is very valid. The premise is that after the Civil War–which to be fair, the first half was pretty historically accurate–ending with a mixed race president, with the cause of reparations to the blacks for their mistreatment. It was filled with clear racism and the basic idea is rather amusing to think of today, but back then, when the Civil War still comparatively fresh was it really so unbelievable? If we use the modern opinions about race and apply them to the film it's easy to be judgmental, but the contemporary attitudes didn't change until *after World War II*. All things considered with the embrace of Victim Culture and the call by black leaders for reparations–maybe film has imitated life to a degree.

CHAPTER THIRTEEN

ENEMIES OF THE POPULIST STATE

T his chapter is to the few who got

it, and most of them at some point didn't always. The people to be discussed either came from left-leaning backgrounds or were outsiders to begin with.

DIRTY TALK

I've never put much stock in heroes or role models and I've made that clear in other writings. However, if I had to choose a role model, it would have to be Mike Rowe. Mike Rowe worked for the Discovery Channel for years as a narrator until he started his own project, *Dirty Jobs*.

His work on *Dirty Jobs* is why he would be my role model. Here's why: The show was Rowe's idea; he not only made it his mission to show some of the most important, untalked about jobs in the country, but he *voluntarily* went out to do them. Anyone, who goes out to some of the worst working environments around, just to direct people's attention to it and say thank you to the hard-working men and women of this country, is an amazing human being.

He went against the popular culture, where bashing the working man is the norm and instead he embraces him. He shows him that his efforts are appreciated and that outside the cultural elite consensus, the working man is still highly respected.

DANA CHANGES HER MIND

Oh Dana Loesch, what are we going to with you! For those who don't know Dana, she is a democrat turned conservative, who is a host of her own show on Glenn Beck's network, The Blaze. She's funny, spunky and highly opinionated and the reason for her changing her mind–she had a family. She realized the damage the democrats were doing to her children's future and decided enough was enough.

Thing is, this has become a common problem with *both* parties, neither want to take the mass abandonment as a sign for some self-evaluation. The massive win by republicans in 2014 of additional seats weren't because there was any faith in them suddenly getting some nerve, as much as being fed up with the democrats. This is where Dana is a strong asset for the limited government movement, she will call you out *no matter what party you belong to.* She is in the same arena as Sean Hannity and Mark Levin, who won't even hesitate to chastise republicans who act against the party's principles.

A CLUELESS GETS A CLUE

Whenever a celebrity publicly

expresses an opinion they have to be prepared for backlash, especially since most of the time it's one that is contrary to the opinions and values of main stream America. It's not only that they don't really know what regular blue-collar people think or believe, it's that they are downright hostile towards those views. Liam Neeson doesn't see anything wrong with decrying gun ownership as "disgraceful" in an interview, or Jim Carrey didn't see anything wrong when he did his internet video, *The Cold Dead Hand*. The same can be said of the Obama enamored Gwyneth Paltrow saying that the president should be given powers to do whatever he wants. These are only a couple of the most insane opinions voiced by the clueless pop culture elite of Hollywood.

There are some who do get it even in the celebrity circles, James Woods has been very vocal about the rampant corruption of the Obamas and has acknowledged that doing so puts his career in jeopardy.

Angelina Jolie, while not exactly a conservative, has been critical of Obama. Oliver Stone–a huge Obama fan–has expressed his concerns about the NSA spying.

So, even in camp Obama things are not always so rosy, but even those with valid complaints will receive social media hate (at times using the same derogatory terminology they claim to find so distasteful). Michelle Malkin's book *UnHinged* is about just that. Clarence Thomas has been called numerous times, by many different people, things like an "Uncle Tom" or other such terms for a racial sell-out. During the 2012 elections, actress Melissa Joan Hart was viciously attacked on Twitter by twits for her opposition to Obama. There is a new comer to the anti-Obama circles that has had to endure the slings and arrows of Obama-ite devotion, the black actress Stacey Dash. In 2008 Dash was an Obama supporter, in 2012 not so much. Happy to have you on our side!

It was because of the Obama political machine that the former co-star of *Clueless* got a clue and turned conservative, but unlike Woods–who thankfully hasn't been hurt professionally by his criticism–hasn't had her career put in harm's way but advanced. She is currently on the Fox network payroll as a regular contributor.

COMING OUT OF THE CAPITALIST CLOSET

If I were to pick the single most dangerous person to the cultural elite, it would be Greg Gutfeld. Gutfeld has quite the story in his journey through political life. He started out as a left wing liberal, in academia going through an illustrious school, then went on to be a Republican then Libertarian. It was in school that he really got converted to the conservative movement, because he knows how to think and that is what makes him dangerous. Even in the bellows of the indoctrination machine he never lost his independence.

He has seen the world of the progressive left and never fully embraced it, so to say he doesn't understand their philosophy would be a false claim. He has seen it first hand and knows how horrible it is. It was the lack of evidence to support their point that Gutfeld condemns. What also makes Gutfeld dangerous is he's genuinely funny, he's very insightful and has a way with words. For progressives this is very bad indeed.

JOHN TAKES ON THE WORLD

John, in this case is John Stossel, the libertarian journalist of Fox Business News. The liberal turned libertarian is the probably the most well know case that a little knowledge can be a dangerous thing for big government supporters. He was getting regular accolades and rewards for his consumer protection reporting, but along the way found something *more* important. He started his career about the same way Ralph Nader did and with the same intentions, but somewhere Nader sold out to the establishment and Stossel started questioning them.

This would be harder than people realize, even for someone like me leaving one of the parties of the duopoly wasn't easy. I live in a mostly conservative state where Libertarians are fairly welcomed. New York is hardly accepting of those not of the hard-core progressive left. Plus Stossel had a well-established career and a lot to lose doing this, but he had to stand by his principles and fortunately it paid off.

WANT TO SEE A MAGIC TRICK

If you were looking for a magic show to take your children to, I wouldn't recommend taking them to see Penn and Teller in Las Vegas, but if I wanted to have a conversation about liberty and a mind opening discussion on atheism, or Libertarianism Penn Jillette would be the man. Most atheists see it as their mission to stop all discussions about God, Penn is eager to engage in it. He might think you're an

idiot for believing in God, but he won't try
to talk you out of it. In fact if you can defend
your point you will have gained a friend.
That's the relationship Penn has with Glenn
Beck. He thinks he's completely "crazy, but
still likes him." This is how an atheist
should be.

TAMMY BREAKS ALL THE RULES

**As confusing as it may be for the
identity** politics crowd to figure out Dana
Loesch or Stacy Dash being conservatives;
Tammy Bruce must really give them a
migraine. Like Dash, Tammy Bruce is a
violation because she fits into two categories
that–to the progressives anyways– should
put her in their camp, she's a woman and
she's gay. Bruce is no progressive though
and takes on the left with full force. So,
when it comes to identity politics Tammy
Bruce belongs to no one.

WE THE LIBERTARIANS

Many misconceptions have been

253

spread about libertarians, unfortunately far too many are from our own making. I'm guilty of this at times myself. I'm against the war on drugs, yet condemn addiction; pro-choice, but question the need for abortion; in favor of marriage equality and gay rights in general, but have no particular affection for the gay lifestyle. I can see why people would be confused. One of the most noteworthy was when I wrote an article defending Paula Dean, for racist comments she made years ago. Outlets that cover her products decided not to cover them afterwards–at least not until the heat from public pressure ended–and I believed that was wrong. She made a mistake and she was being punished for it almost thirty years later.

Recently, the University of Oklahoma suspended the fraternity Sigma Alpha Epsilon house for a racist chant performed on a bus. The president of the university was "shocked and disappointed ... by the outright display of racism displayed .... and

254

we have zero tolerance for racism." The group Unheard, posted the video on the internet, which includes in the chant the line "there will never be a nigger at SAE." For the record, I find racism to be morally wrong and just plain disgusting but the actions of the school were excessive. Breaking up a fraternity is an extreme overreaction for a violation of misconduct. Why is it appropriate for a school to take such a stance while an employer is held hostage by affirmative action laws? Why is it tolerable to be intolerant to others' points of view and take such radical actions, in the name of "diversity?"

Diversity means many different opinions, but whenever a contrary one is brought it up its owner is accused of racism or sexism. The example of Sigma Alpha is clearly racist, but so what? Should their free speech really be violated, or worse, suffer lifetime consequences because of a moment of stupidity on a YouTube Video? See, that's how it's still morally coherent, to be disgusted with the thoughts and actions of individuals making racial remarks, but defend those that made them. The overreaction by the school board to Sigma Alpha and the retail outlets with Dean, are unequal to their actions. That's what is wrong with Victim Culture and identity politics in general. They demand reparations by those who did nothing wrong to them; the reparations demanded are vastly outweighed by the crime; or they ask for reparations done to past generations that occurred long before they were even alive.

CHAPTER FOURTEEN

CONCLUDING REMARKS

So what do we take from all this? Is **America** an angry, hate-filled, nation of bigots, or is it still a land of unbridled opportunity for those willing to get their hands dirty?

WE'RE ALL VICTIMS NOW

Alright, so let's take a moment and **review,** in the long list of Victim Culture and identity politics we have the following:

Blacks hate America for slavery and the mistreatment of the blacks brought to the continent as slaves; they were property and not people —in the eyes of

the Europeans and early colonialists–and were raped and beaten. In the contemporary context, blacks are harassed by the police and victims of laws like "stand your ground." While black people were treated in an objectionable manner in the past, that weak argument is advanced so they can get "freebies" from the federal piggy bank. They work hard–in the form of protest–for their entitlements but not to get valid employment. They work hard for abortion, so their recreational sex will not have any consequences. They struggle for subsidized housing and SNAP payments without realizing that these programs enslave them to the government more than any slave master their relatives had. Anyone who calls for reason and restraint in federal spending is branded a racist for their troubles. Rather than embrace the positive examples of Booker T. Washington and Frederick Douglass, they look to Jesse Jackson and Louis Farrakhan.

Mexicans and Native American tribes

say we owe them for "stealing their lands." We didn't steal it, it was taken from tribes who took it from *other* tribes long before the Europeans landed here. They also use myth to justify taking it back, we don't owe them anything.

The ladies say that all men and mankind are evil and need to be neutered or killed. History–and even some feminists–say this is a harsh and unfair characterization of men. As Camille Paglia, the feminist writer put it, "Masculinity is aggressive, unstable, combustible. It is also the most creative cultural force in history…it is patriarchal society that has freed me as a woman. It is capitalism that has given me the leisure to sit at this desk writing… Let us stop being small-minded about men and freely acknowledge what treasure their obsessiveness has poured into culture." We acknowledge that it was men who have created the world we have now, imperfect yes, but so is all of the human race.

Environmental and animal rights radicals claim that we are destroying the planet and killing off every animal on it. The environmental and anti-animal cruelty movement has lost its way. Rather than going after legitimate concerns, they waste their time trying to bring in new regulations and hurting businesses and individuals. In the end putting their very causes in jeopardy.

Warring theological factors deride each other, stating they have moral superiority–proving their *inferiority*. The different religions; whether it be a form of Christianity, Muslim, or Atheist, need to work on their interactions. Atheists and Muslims, you have no right to commit violence on Christians or have their religious symbols removed or destroyed. Christians, evolution has some inconsistencies in the theory but strong evidence to back it up, and ignoring that science connected to it just makes you a Santorum or Huckabee. Don't be a Santorum or Huckabee!

Anti-capitalist progressives cling to the failed ideologies of the past –reinventing modern versions of socialism and ignoring the atrocities and ramifications of such movements. The crux of Victim Culture, the need to dismantle capitalism. The socialists condemn the inefficiencies of capitalism without acknowledging the problems in the state. Historically speaking, socialism has never worked and it seems to be that it's just a bad idea all around.

We have seen the hints of future victimhood. As if all the rest isn't enough, we have seen what should be expected at some point in time, victim status against the unattractive, the smelly and pedophiles. While we're at it how about those who taste bad, of course that will lead to the counter-suits of "being licked" but I'm sure there are enough lawyers to go around.

CUI BONO

It's interesting to see one of your books play out in real life, unfortunately, the wrong one went from fiction to fact. Of my fictional books it would have been preferred to see *'We the Rodents'* become policy more than *LEGACY*, but with the Ebola scare that's what happened. The whole thing played out as the "historical event" in my book–a mutated variant of the black plague is unleashed on the populace, with a state of emergency called and the government takes over–aside from the disease being Ebola, the Obama administration's reaction was different, and a bit puzzling. In fact it was the polar opposite–rather than demanding action and federal intervention he called for cooler heads to prevail. Did he use up all his indignation on Trayvon? This doesn't make sense until you examine the full picture–so what was his reasons for such a timid response?

First, is his animosity based on a political bias–that was obvious; the second, his bias as a racial instigator–that was more subtle. The GOP had pushed for action with the initial outbreak of the disease demanding travel restrictions and extended quarantine procedures. We have seen that the Obama administration doesn't have a problem with travel restrictions or violating people traveling for that matter–so the obvious answer here is that it must be because it would make the republicans look bad. If the democrats had called for these measures, he would have acquiesced to post haste, but not to those mean republicans. The other reason for what he did was to appease his race friends, remember, that to Al Sharpton Ebola is a "race issue" not to be openly discussed and agreeing with Sharpton will score big points with "his people." That's only part of the racial component here, if travel restrictions were employed that would be detrimental to his immigration policies. Obama wants to court as many Mexican immigrants as possible to add them to the democratic rosters, letting them come in without any restrictions and granting them entitlements–or bribes–is the only way to do that.

Based on their cultural values, Mexicans would actually be more inclined to vote republican. This policy of bribes and emotional manipulation are the only real way the social democrats have been able to continue. Wouldn't that make it a guaranteed victory for the republicans? No, because establishment republicans aren't any better than the social democrats. Rather than standing up, they work with the democrats making it a party of one, they have their own special interest groups and don't want to be called a bigot by the progressive elite, so it benefits them more to play along.

So who benefits from all this lack of contention? The social democrats for starters, but not the hard working voters, just the extremists. The radicals: the feminists, the green eco-terrorists, the class-warfare anti-capitalists, the race agitators, the union godfathers and any others in the lists of special interest groups, lobbyists and politicians, who wouldn't hesitate selling their own mother into government slavery–aka entitlements.

When people bring up entitlements one of the biggest criticisms is tied to immigrants–who are not only stealing our jobs, but get entitlements from the government. Unions were capitalizing on this fear for years and now embrace the foreigners and only focusing on entitlement programs for illegal immigrants makes it sound like you're fine with natural born citizens or legal immigrants scamming the system. This plays right into the hands of the enablers, keeping the nation divided and angry at each other without an opportunity for an open debate. I'm not saying that it's right for illegal immigrants to get special privileges, but that it's wrong for *anyone* to get special privileges. With the current broken system of entitlements we have, it's not always clear who benefits, but it is who suffers–the American public.

WHAT DID OBAMA DO FOR YOU?

In the February issue of the progressive *Mother Jones* magazine, writer Chris Mooney posted a question "Are you a racist?" in which the author discusses his meeting with a doctor to take the Implicit Association Test (IAT). This test is supposed to demonstrate how racist you are with a word association, if you mentally associate "bad" terminology to someone who's black, clearly you have at least some animosity or mistrust towards those of African descent. In other words, if you hate Obama and associate terms like "socialist" or "progressive" towards him and view those as bad, than this test conclusively shows you're a racist. Right!–another conclusion you could make is that his race *doesn't matter* and you hate him for being a progressive. That's more my case.

He's the hipster, "rock star" president, he chides everything great about this nation and hates those who disagree with him. He made promise after promise and has broken the only ones that I would have agreed with him on. He didn't balance the budget, in fact he fought to make sure *that didn't happen.* He and Eric Holder took a weak step on the war on drugs pardoning a few thousand rather than taking real steps of reform, yes, they were released but under the Federal law *even in states where marijuana is legal* the DOJ can *still* arrest these men again for drug charges. For some reason some thought Obama was going to get special interests and lobbyists out of Washington, he didn't. He is perfectly comfortable with lobbyists and wouldn't make a move without asking special interests activists if it were okay. He hasn't closed the Guantanamo Bay detention center, his argument being that he couldn't get congress to side with him. Did his magic pen run out of ink? About the only promise he did fulfill was the Affordable Care Act.

In regards to marriage equality he gets that wrong too. In a statement he said: "I have to tell you that over the course of several years, as I talk to friends and family and neighbors ... members of my own staff ... committed, in monogamous ... same-sex relationships, who are raising kids ... these are soldiers ... out there fight[ing] on my behalf and ... feel[ing] constrained, even now that Don't Ask, Don't Tell is gone, because they're not able to commit themselves in marriage... I've just concluded ... that I think same-sex should be able to get married." With the current environment in the government being so hostile to those who oppose gay marriage, it's highly unlikely that the Obama's modus operandi in this policy is going to shift. Rather than encourage churches to no longer accept federal marriage, he's more comfortable fostering contention between gay rights activists and traditional marriage advocates, making sure to scorch the middle ground in the issue.

If there was any statement that encompasses the Obama ideology of government largesse it would have to be this one: "After more than a decade of war, it's time to focus on nation building here at home. As a new greatest generation returns from overseas, we must ask ourselves, what kind of country will they come back to? Will it be a country where a shrinking number of Americans do really well while a growing number barely get by? Or will it be a country where everyone gets a fair shot, everyone does their fair share, and everyone plays by the same set of rules —a country with opportunity worthy of the troops that protect us?" A pretty speech right from the FDR playbook. One thing is for sure, he has made a lot of promises and the first one he broke was that he was going to work with others to unite the country. He has proven not to be a victim of America, but one of the worst of its progressive bullies.

MRS JEKYLL CREATED MR HYDE

Remember the Ray Rice incident? Rice beats his wife in an elevator and every news outlets covers it—and over-covers it! That's not to say his actions were appropriate–no one should be treated that way, but his wife shouldn't have struck him either. What was bizarre was many normally logical, rational people tried to dismiss her part in what happened. They said that since he's a man he should just take it. Just like Lorena Bobbitt, the guilt goes both ways, she had no right to strike him.

Now wait a minute, you berated the athletes for being whiners earlier– how is this different? First off, Rice was struck by his wife, someone who he should have felt totally comfortable and safe around. In his career Rice was surely conditioned to endure a level of "abusive" behavior; but at home it's a different situation it's supposed to be a sanctuary. Secondly, the "crybaby" athletes I was chastising weren't *physically* assaulted but verbally taunted *with online posts*. This is just one more example of our nations' double-standards and it's demonstrating–yet again–that it's usually the "perpetrator" that is the *real* victim. Men have to put up with this from feminists all the time. Men are jerks, and deserve their mistreatment but what about the guys who are not jerks? The feminists don't make a distinction between the two and this has lasting consequences for our society. When the non-jerks are cussed out for crimes they didn't even commit, they are turned into the "guy who doesn't call you." If Mr. Nice-guy is categorized as a jerk he might as well have done something to deserve it!

In their war on boys in school–claiming that boys have such advantages–they have left boys to fend for themselves. The girls don't need help, it's the boys that do and because of women's irrational fears of boys turning into men–who are sure to sexually assault them, they justify their heartless campaign against them. It's the boys that need more help in schools and should be encouraged to extend their education past high school, the girls already are far ahead in both. It's the boys that would benefit most from same-sex education, yet when such measures are considered it's exclusively for the girls, since they are owed reparations. In 1994 Senator John Danforth proposed same-sex classes after seeing the U.S. Research has shown that same-sex classes are beneficial for both genders, but particularly for boys. The amendment passed the Senate but the house rejected it. Danforth comments on the results, "I was stunned at the organized opposition to the amendment. Opponents argued ... the provision would result in injustice to young girls, despite the ... requirement that same-sex classes be offered to both boys and girls." One of those critics the group NOW argued that such a bill would be tantamount to racial segregation and just as harmful. Anne Connors, president of the New York chapter comments that "public money should not be used to fund institutions segregated on the basis of sex." So when is the UN Women's funding going to get cut?

Christina Hoff Summers ha this to say about such thinking in *The War Against Boys*, that "the gender theorists and activists

... have recently begun to tell us boys too need attention–not because schools are neglecting their academic needs but because 'under patriarchy,' males are socialized to destructive masculine ideals ... experts at Harvard, Wellesley and Tufts ... believe that boys and men ... will remain sexist ... unless socialized away from conventional maleness. It may be too late to change adult men: boys ... are still salvageable... As one keynote speaker at a convention of gender-equality experts, pointed out to her audience, 'We have an incredible opportunity. Kids are so malleable.'"

The National Women's Law Center hasn't been subtle in its opinion that little girls are owed reparations. Deborah Burke, serving as Senior Counsel of the group, commented that "in light of discrimination against women in education and the barriers that female students continue to face based on their gender, there [may be] a legitimate place for such programs." Judith Shapiro, the president of Barnard College topped that in a 1994 op-ed for the *Baltimore Sun*: "In a society that favor men .... men's institutions operate to preserve privilege, women's institutions challenge privilege and attempt to expand access to the good things of life." As long as they have been a victim, at least. The truth is they haven't been the victim, at least not in modern times.

In Prince George's County, Maryland the educators tried to establish the "Black Male Achievement Initiative" to help the boys who were "at the bottom in every respect, in academic ... [and] social development," as one school board member put it. The proposal was rebuffed because it was "short changing female students, and we're not going to do that anymore," stated a thrilled board member. The New York City public schools successfully established an elite school such as what was proposed in Prince George's County, but it was an all-girl school. In 1996 the Young Women's Leadership School, an all-girl school in East Harlem opened its doors. The *New York*

Times and others urged the school Chancellor Rudy Crew to establish a "similar island of excellence for boys." His response to the *Times* was "this is a case where the existence of the all-girls school makes an important statement about the viable education of girls." Somehow an equivalent one for boys negates that?

All the evidence points to boys needing more help, including the CDC. According to Mary Pipher in *Reviving Ophelia*, "The Center for Disease Control in Atlanta reports … the suicide rate among children age ten to fourteen rose 75 percent between 1979 and 1988 … a look at the sex breakdown of the CDC's suicide statistics reveals … for males … the suicide rate increased 71 percent between 1979 and 1988; for girls the increase was 27 percent."

The view of the radical feminists, as summed up by Sandra Lee Bartky, a feminist philosopher, is that "human beings are born 'bisexual' and conditioned through patriarchal society, into male and female gender personalities, the one destined to command, the other to obey." If that is indeed truly the case, the feminists have it wrong on who is subservient. Men acquiesce to women all the time, even in the White House it has historically been the First Lady who calls the shots. What the feminists are really trying to do is turn the male populace into eunuchs. They hold up as their iconoclasts, women like: Lorena Bobbitt, Jodi Arias and the Femitheist, women so angry that nothing less than archaic torture similar to that in the Middle Ages would suffice.

These actions are hurting the whole of society so, this would mean the feminists themselves are creating a perpetual cycle of abuse on not only men, *but on women.* If that is indeed the case–as my findings seem to indicate–the "War on Women" really is nothing more than a propaganda campaign for women victimhood.

JUST DON'T CARE

Republican or democrat, both have a similar basic manner in making their decisions, they lead with their feelings. Republicans decide according to their religious virtues and democrats according to the tenets of compassion. Understand, I'm not being critical of either, but on their obsession to make everyone else conform to their individual stances of morality; and part of my criticism is for their own good as well. How many times have religious overtones been used on either side to advance a cause? Remember the social gospel movement or the temperance era? Sojourner Truth and others who wanted to advance the progressive agendas of social justice, did so using religious sermons.

When someone like Bill O'Reilly spouts off figures saying that 10 or 15% of the populace admits to being non-denominational or not Christian I can't help but think–*So the hell what?* Just because they aren't religious, doesn't mean they are unethical; and just because they religious doesn't mean they are, look at Harry Reid or Rick Santorum, very religious not very ethical. Or Mike Huckabee, he might live according to theological principles, but he has no ethics. The best example is Barack Obama, he joined a Christian church, not out of the need of faith, but out of political expediency. His wife isn't much better, saying that "to anyone who says that church is no place to talk about the issues you tell them there is no better place ... these are not just political issues–they are moral ones."

When it comes to the exercise of the law neither approach is valid, they care too much about caring–or at least showing others they care–and not about actually finding solutions. Both think that government can fix the problem, no matter what it is and both have lost faith in the American people. I haven't; and most of that comes from the fact that I just don't care. When I hear about a hurricane ravaging Florida, I feel for the Floridians, but I don't think that we should send FEMA in to help them. If we get rid of FEMA and get rid of any laws that stand in the way–I don't know what they are, but there are sure to be a law or two (hundred) to inhibit it–then someone else could step in and assist them. *There's no guarantee that someone would do that.* You're right, but how good a job did FEMA do after such disasters? Not great. How about solving the problem of police misconduct? Many libertarians subscribe to the idea that the police and even the courts should be privatized. Some cities already have volunteer police and as far as the courts are concerned, a privatized court is a provocative idea that is worth exploration. That doesn't mean we should rush to abandon the current justice system, but it couldn't hurt to consider other options.

MISTRIAL

In chapter seven I brought up the Earps and the gunfight at the OK Corral, in which I intimated the Earps were in the same league as the callous officers abusing their power on YouTube videos. That's because I intentionally left out part of the story–until now. The reported reason for the OK corral fight was that the Earps went to disarm the Cowboys for the illegal act of carrying guns in town. There was more to the story–the Cowboys were infamous criminals in the area, tolerated only because they brought money into the town of Tombstone. Earlier, the day of the OK Corral incident, one of the Cowboys was wandering the town–in a drunken rage– shouting that he was going to kill the Earp brothers.

The townspeople wanted the Earps to intervene but turned on them afterward. The sleeping media of Tombstone claimed the Cowboys were the victims and they even got the town to try to hang the brothers for murder! The end result for the Earps, history vindicates them and the corruption of the Tombstone legal system is revealed, proving the Earps to be heroes. This didn't happen until towards the end of Wyatt Earp's life, however, not until his biography was written in the 1930's. That's when the legend changes in favor of the Earps. This is why it's so important that we have full disclosure of history, if not the true story of Wyatt Earp and Billy the Kid–fighters against their local oligarchies–would have been written unfavorably by those who wanted to keep out those who threatened their system of power.

DISCRIMINATIONS ARE A NECESSARY EVIL

Each and every day we make choices; do I go to work or call out sick; do I have a salad or pizza for dinner; do I spend my money on this or that, and many are made without any thought about the preference given to one choice over the other. That's how it should be, we shouldn't have to stress out over how someone else might feel about the choices we make.

Oh, you picked a salad over pizza–you

must be anti-pizza, or anti-Italian. Since pizza, as we are familiar with the United States, isn't really an Italian dish, this argument has a certain amount of logical disconnect–but no less some of the other arguments presented by activists in this book!

You spent your money on a US made product, you must be against foreigners. For some people that might be the case, for others it's pride in their country. My decisions are made based on quality of the product and price, sometimes that means it comes from the US, sometimes it doesn't. But the argument here is that the US needs all these rules against foreign markets to keep an edge; but if we want to be a free country again we have to *fully* embrace the free market, not pick and choose what parts should be free and what should not. That picking and choosing is one of the ways we have gotten into trouble in the first place– because like so many other times –it has invited government to get involved where it doesn't belong.

You're going to work: you're an evil capitalist that hates minorities, children, women, the elderly and gays. Close, I am an ardent capitalist, but I'm not evil and I don't hate others because of their personal choices. I condemn their conduct only when it affects me or those I care about.

These are just a small sample of the decisions we make all the time and yes; I exaggerated in the ways others react to those choices, or did I? When you talk about animals being allowed to sue you, or artisans eating lobster on the public dole, or the contempt by climate scientists towards those who want hard evidence of man's influence on the planet; is it really so far out there? Every day we make choices– discriminations, if you will– about who we let into our lives, what we do with our bodies and financial decisions which someone, somewhere, will disagree with. That's fine, but that doesn't give them the right to stop you from making the decision.

The social busy-bodies–politicians, lobbyists, temperance advocates and other activists–believe they do; and the only way to stop them is to choose not to give in. Don't let them silence you by taking your voice of choice.

CLOSING ARGUMENTS

Your Honor, ladies and gentlemen of the jury (you the reader) let's be completely honest what this Victims Culture movement really is–the concise and total exorcising of the capitalist system to replace it with a quasi-socialist, progressive alternative. In the eyes of people like Barack Obama and his ilk, that's the only way to an egalitarian system. Problem is, we already have an egalitarian system in place and so many people have proven that. Jay-Z and Azealia Banks might be critical of the capitalist system, but they are where they are today because of capitalism. There's not many other countries where you start out poor, completely destitute and end up a millionaire–let alone doing so by being openly critical of the government or its representatives. In a lot of countries that will get you jailed if you're *lucky*!

To be fair to the anti-capitalists claims, not everyone ends up that way, many fail at the attempts of success. That's an argument of equal results, not equal opportunities and we all have equal opportunities for success in America. Equality of results is highly over-rated and doesn't end up the way most think it does, everyone will be equal–an equal share of poverty! Actually even equal results aren't true in progressive systems. Socialist and communists nations still have a class structure with those that have and those that have not. At least in a capitalist society, that's an open declaration and not a state secret. In a capitalist system everyone needs to work for what you get, in a socialist you have to work too, but you never really get to *keep what you get.* You don't own anything, the government does and if you step out of line–watch out!

See, this is what I find to be the most befuddling of all–in regards to Victim Culture–the compartmentalization, the cries of the inherent evils of the greedy capitalists and the "good intentions" benevolence of government. The latter, being one the longest-running social myths. As much as the progressives–of either side–want to herald their version of big government as the answer, that's difficult to validate when examined in any kind of impartial way. In order for that to be true–you would have to ignore the fact that so much of the corruption of business is due to the laws established by the federal government; who conveniently use business leaders as scapegoats for their own incompetence. That's not to say that businessmen act in the right all the time, but it's a little confusing trading one conglomerate that is beholden to public opinion, for one that habitually skirts such criticism. In other words, those who have total hatred for corporate entities, are putting their faith in the biggest conglomerate, corporate entity of all–the United States government.

NOT GUILTY

As I hope I've shown, the US didn't commit any hate crimes. Strictly speaking "hate crimes" are illegal, seeing as these statutes are a violation of the first amendment. But besides that, the claims are untrue, it wasn't white people or America that are victimizing everyone. It's not whites who cause most of the damage to the black communities–with the exception of white progressives that carry out "white guilt" laws of reparations–mostly it's other blacks killing black youth in urban areas. It's poverty and failing public schools, that keep them in the inner cities where they can't grow.

Mexicans are not hurt by the immigration system–unless they try to get in legally–but illegals are hurt by the coyote smugglers, who enslave them, rape them and murder them at the slightest provocation.

Native American activists push for more government money for their reservations, despite the evidence that suggests that it keeps them–along with basically every other social demographic, using such resources– living in squalor.

Feminists do far more harm to women than men do, they may claim the counter culture for creating an environment of hostility towards women, but the evidence shows that they are responsible for this animosity. Out of their fear of men, they have taken it upon themselves to destroy everything about little boys–in turn making them very confused and more aggressive. This–in turn–puts women in more danger.

Most of the cases of whites and "hate crimes" in regards to victims of extreme violence, were when the minority instigated the crime. When the violence was perpetrated by a white person, it was by an authority figure of law enforcement and race doesn't seem to be the major factor. A study of the Ferguson police suggests there's a racial bias against blacks in the area, that might be true, but without examining the study itself it should be viewed with reservations. The study itself could be biased, or flawed with the questions asked. If it's proven valid, then an investigation into the cause of racial bias in Ferguson should proceed. They could be practicing more racial profiling there because of a higher statistic average of crimes in the black communities of Ferguson. If it has a high poverty and government housing that could be a cause; increased poverty equals increased crime, and more police who abuse its citizens. In poorer areas police can make more arrests, simply because the residents can't afford legal counsel. Or it could be that Ferguson, simply got the bad end when it comes to higher than normal power-hungry police. Whatever the problem–or exaggerated problem–may be, the town of Ferguson is not the representation of the whole United States.

Freedom Rider, Frank Thomas said–at a

speaking engagement for WSU, "The country is light years away from where it was in 1956." He's very right; if you take an objective analysis of the progress–*real* progress– made since the sixties in opportunities for all social classes the improvement is quite impressive. Many professions that once were not available to women, homosexuals, or minorities–in some cases with legal barriers–now have full participation of all. We have female tattoo artists, politicians and scientists. We have a woman human cannonball, Gemma Kirby, with the Ringling Brothers Circus, and recently the first black woman, Loretta Lynch, was sworn in as Attorney General. Progressives try to take credit for all this and at the same time diminish it; but the truth is, their efforts have once again proven to be a barricade to social progress. According to government data, advancement opportunities for minorities and women were already shifting and their intervention caused that shift to stagnate. If the feminists really cared about women, why didn't they stand up for Cytherea, the former porn star raped in her Las Vegas home? The feminists were silent because her attackers were black, not the typical "rape culture" attacker's profile of "the rich white man" according to journalist Matt Forney. There could be some truth to that.

If they really cared about "protecting women's choices" why were they so hostile towards Ann Romney and Kaley Cuoco, for wanting to have a "traditional" family life? Or stand behind Carrie Prejean, Miss CA of 2009 for stating her opinion of gay marriage? Prejean made the statement: "Well, I think it's great that Americans are able to choose one way or the other. We live in a land where you can choose same-sex marriage or opposite marriage... I believe that marriage should be between a man and woman, no offense to anyone out there." Apparently she did offend one person, social commentator Perez Hilton called her a "dumb bitch" for her comments. *She wasn't even being critical* of gay marriage, she was stating her *opinion* that it was morally wrong.

If racial agitators really cared, and "Black Lives Mattered", then why would they not try to discourage the rioting and looting *before* it happens. When they fan the flames of "righteous indignation" in race relations, instead they don't draw any distinctions in the proper style of peaceful protest and that of terrorizing *their own communities*. What about the business owners of Ferguson who are black? Their lives clearly don't matter! But why make this an issue of race anyway, why isn't it simply "Lives Matter?" If America is "guilty" of anything at all, it is being far too tolerant of such rampant, open intolerance.

MY CONFESSION

It's only appropriate that I end this book with a confession–I did not want to write this book. All the previous written works had a certain amount of enjoyment to it as well as the pertinent need for it, in this case that enjoyment was lacking. I wrote this book because it had to be written. When the Trayvon Martin shooting occurred, I tried to sit back and wait for it to blow over–instead, it blew up! Then Michael Brown was shot in Ferguson, Eric Garner was suffocated in New York and Freddie Gray in Baltimore. These are but a few of the many numerous examples–in our most recent past alone–of the history of identity politics and Victim Culture claims of the United States. Which is part of the problem, there is far too much material. If I wanted to, this book could easily be over a thousand pages, but I didn't want to contribute to our national suicide numbers. For me, the subject of social victimhood is not only incredibly manipulative, but downright infuriating. There's no logical analysis behind it and it's all about emotional manipulation; which creates this logic vacuum, where truth can't survive so debate consists simply of screaming.

Ultimately, I hate identity politics because by its very nature, it polarizes the country on superfluous biological traits rather than on division based on contrary ideas and philosophies. Hearing stories like Shirley Sherrod, who had a "moral dilemma" based on skin color of someone asking for her assistance. Sherrod said, at a NAACP meeting, she "… was struggling with the fact that so, many black people had lost their farm lands. And here [she] was faced with having to help a white person save their land. So [she] didn't give him her full force …. [but] did enough." The farmer didn't begrudge her this but was grateful, I can't be generous, however, because such mentality has become the norm. Not only did she game the system and face no genuine repercussions for this– other than by the late, great Andrew Breitbart of course–but her "apology" was rife with anti-capitalist innuendoes, about it not being about race but in the end doing it for the "little guy". Yeah that's much better!

Or when I hear the pro-Obama diatribe from progressive blowhards, like Eric Alterman–who is just as enamored with Bill De Blasieo and wants to curl up and cuddle with both of them, it makes me cringe! He's up there with Chris Hedges on the nausea scale of boredom in writing–with nothing compelling or even accidently interesting to say–more of the standard anti-American, anti-capitalist claptrap. Maybe they should start a magazine with feminist Amanda Marcotte.

The Obama love fest continues with Dr. Peggy Drexler making the very unbiased comparison of the Romney/Obama Presidential race of 2012, as "Obama has deftly offered a choice: a respectful and inclusive voice of the future, versus a scholarly tormentor (Romney) aligned with the intolerant voices of the past." Or a professor at Princeton's, Center for African-American Studies, Iman Perry, "I think many white Americans are fearful with Obama in the White House ... that the racial balance of power is shifting. And that's frightening ... because people are always afraid to give up power ... some liberals have long maintained that racism requires power, and so black people can't be racist." Even when they are in a position of power "liberals" can't be happy, especially when they believe they are "owed" by the country.

Toure of MSNBC, commented that "there is basic, lesser humanity generally ascribed to black people, even one this alpha (talking about Obama), this much in power, this much in control." Joe Williams of Politico describes Obama's racial challenges as it being "very, very difficult to place race outside of the context. Mostly because a lot of the interruptions, a lot of the disrespect has been unprecedented. We haven't seen anything like this before." Did you forget the reporter that kept interrupting Reagan until he had to tell him to sit down and shut up, or all the nasty comments from celebrities about President Bush? This is not "unprecedented" that's why our nation has not instituted the sedition acts, not once but multiple times. That's why the progressive left has been so eager to beef up Net Neutrality. This group of Obama-ites don't care that people are being critical of the president, but because they are being critical of *their* president. It doesn't dawn on them that a "fair Share" of the nation is no longer in love with Obama.

This infatuation with blacks is nothing new for the contemporary social democrats, they have to make up for the policies of Andrew Jackson, Andrew Johnson and Woodrow Wilson. That's why they elected the very hip-hop president Barack Obama, who along with the works of Saul Alinsky and Karl Marx, has probably also read the classics of "Iceberg Slim" like, *PIMP: The Story of My Life.* Or the memoir of Donald Goines, *Dopefiend.* Or the lionizing of Trayvon by Michael Eric Dyson of MSNBC: "Now it is the case that whatever hoods we wear, sagging pants, those become part of the folklore of American racism because it now signifies to white America that this a hood, this is a thug, and the suspicion that is cast not only on Trayvon Martin." Or the lionizing of the Black Panthers by intellectual Tom Wolfe, "*These are no civil-rights* negroes *wearing grey suits three sizes too big*–no more interminable Urban League banquets in hotel rooms where they try to alternate blacks and whites around the table as if they were stringing Arapaho beads–these are real men! Shoot-outs, revolutions, pictures in *Life* magazine of police-men grabbing Black Panthers like they were Vietcong–somehow it all runs together in the head with the whole thing of how *beautiful* they are." At the retirement of Jon Stewart from *The Daily Show*, Lizz Wistead of MSNBC was "just glad Trevor Noah (Stewart's replacement) was not another white guy."

This is how the world is shaping up, feminists, racial agitators, environmentalists, gay rights advocates and other anti-capitalists, all trying to change the world without regard for anyone else or whether the policy ideas are improvements. With this vacuum of "social tolerance" it should be no surprise we get people like Issa Rae, who think that black people are still misrepresented on TV or that even a few of the organizations that do good have to identify themselves under identity political terms; take the educational activist groups 100 Black Men of America Inc. and Black Girls Code. Both groups do amazing work to encourage participation of black youth to make their lives better economically and to make them financially secure. Both do genuine compassionate works to help those who are struggling the most, but both are still born out of cultural insolation. **The mission of the 100 Black Men of America Inc., is to improve the quality of the life within our communities and enhance educational and economic opportunities for all African Americans.** That's great, but why be so inclusive? All our children are at risk because of the nation's failing public education system, why single out only *black* youth?

Kimberly Bryant the founder of Black Girls Code talks about her experience in college, of "feeling culturally insolated" because "few of her class mates looked like her" and "there's much to be said for making any challenging journey with people of the same cultural background."

"Much has changed since my college days, but there's still a dearth of African-American women in science, technology, engineering and most professions, an absence that cannot be explained by ... a lack of interest in these fields. Lack of access and lack of exposure to STEM topics are the likelier culprits.

"By launching Black Girls Code, I hope to provide young and preteen girls of color opportunities to learn in-demand skills in technology and computer programming at a time when they are naturally thinking about what they want to be when they grow up."

With all due respect to Kimberly Bryant, the way to fight cultural insolation, is not to give in to it, but to go out and broaden your horizons. I can't relate to Bryant, I've never felt a real need to gravitate towards others based on superficial traits, but on whether I found them interesting or not. If I'm prejudice against anyone, it would be the boring and the logically anemic. There's never been anyone that I felt was of the same "cultural background," at least not in the manner Bryant is inferring. Now don't get me wrong, I'm not being critical of either of these organizations or what they do. I think they perform a great service, unlike so many others that I've covered throughout the book. It's the need for "cultural insolation" that I'm being critical of, because in the end, that is what has been the cause of all this mess. People feel the need to be "with their own kind" and the progressive enablers manipulate that to advance their own goals.

Eric Holder referred to the United States as "a nation of cowards," when it comes to race relations. Are we "a nation of cowards," when it comes to feminism too, or the environment? Are we "a nation of cowards" when it comes to lawsuit abuse and cronyism? If we are "a nation of cowards" then it is because we have been beaten down by people like Eric Holder and the American public is tired. This is the worst thing about Victim Culture, it doesn't matter how much you discuss it, it doesn't make things any better. Someone will become offended and the discussion will end. In the "nation of cowards" the only cowards I see are the ones surrounding the Obama administration.

RECOMMENDED READING

30 Seconds Economics   Donald Marron

Bankrupt   David Limbaugh

Bullies   Ben Shapiro

Dark History: The Popes   Brenda Ralph Lewis

Designer Genes   Steven Potter P.H.D.

Dreamers and Deceivers   Glenn Beck

EntreLeadership   Dave Ramsey

George Washington on Leadership
Richard Brookhiser

Ghetto Nation   Cora Daniels

Liberal Facism   Jonah Goldberg

Miracles and Massacres   Glenn Beck

More Shocking Secrets of American History
Bill Coate

Not Cool   Greg Gutfeld

Sergeant Rex   Mike Dowling

Stupid Liberals   Leland Gregory

The New Reagan Revolution   Michael Reagan

The War Against Boys   Christina Hoff Summers

APPENDIX: SAVE THE CLEVELAND INDIANS

This is the photo I sent out.

AMERICANUS LIBERTAE

Follow On you tube
twitter and rss
wordpress.com